Positive Thinking

Calm Your Thoughts & Eliminate Negative Thinking

(How to Stop Focusing on Nonsense and Live a Better Life)

Robert Brown

Published By **Hailey Leigh**

Robert Brown

All Rights Reserved

Positive Thinking: Calm Your Thoughts & Eliminate Negative Thinking (How to Stop Focusing on Nonsense and Live a Better Life)

ISBN 978-1-7386412-9-1

No part of this guidebook shall be reproduced in any form without permission in writing from the publisher except in the case of brief quotations embodied in critical articles or reviews.

Legal & Disclaimer

The information contained in this book is not designed to replace or take the place of any form of medicine or professional medical advice. The information in this book has been provided for educational & entertainment purposes only.

The information contained in this book has been compiled from sources deemed reliable, and it is accurate to the best of the Author's knowledge; however, the Author cannot guarantee its accuracy and validity and cannot be held liable for any errors or omissions. Changes are periodically made to this book. You must consult your doctor or get professional medical advice before using any of the suggested remedies, techniques, or information in this book.

Upon using the information contained in this book, you agree to hold harmless the Author from and against any damages, costs, and expenses, including any legal fees potentially resulting from the application of any of the information provided by this guide. This disclaimer applies to any damages or injury caused by the use and application, whether directly or indirectly, of any advice or information presented, whether for breach of contract, tort, negligence, personal injury, criminal intent, or under any other cause of action.

You agree to accept all risks of using the information presented inside this book. You need to consult a professional medical practitioner in order to ensure you are both able and healthy enough to participate in this program.

Table Of Contents

Chapter 1: The Process of Positive Thought 1

Chapter 2: Advantages of Maintaining an Upbeat Attitude 12

Chapter 3: Exaggeratedly Negative 25

Chapter 4: Dedicate Regular Time to Your Passions 36

Chapter 5: Creating an Emotional Safe Zone 47

Chapter 6: Creating a Bright Future 61

Chapter 7: Observing Other People 69

Chapter 8: Understanding the Impact of Thoughts 72

Chapter 9: Cultivating A Positive Mindset 85

Chapter 10: The Power of Gratitude 102

Chapter 11: Cultivating Optimism Finding the Silver Lining 111

Chapter 12: Setting Clear and Inspiring Goals 118

Chapter 13: Aligning Thoughts and Behavior 135

Chapter 14: Understanding the Science of Positivity 140

Chapter 15: Overcoming Negative Thought Patterns 148

Chapter 16: Cultivating a Positive Mindset 153

Chapter 17: Nurturing Positive Relationships 157

Chapter 18: Creating a Positive Environment 166

Chapter 19: Understanding Success 175

Chapter 1: The Process Of Positive Thought

There is a deep-seated enjoy of delight that arises while you take into account your personal desires and the way with the aid of the usage of that you can satisfy them. This pleasure empowers you to take price of your existence. It's as despite the fact that your thoughts releases endorphins, which make you sense pleasure and happiness, when you think about some element or a person that makes you happy. These are the gadgets that assist the boom of a high-quality outlook in us.

Numerous psychological researches have showed that happy people possess a completely unique trait that permits them to stay better lives than unhappy ones. What do you expect the motive of that is? Okay, it's far an easy one Hopefulness.

The beautiful component about optimism is that it's far a talent you can accumulate. In every exceptional context, all it takes to cultivate superb questioning in oneself is to encompass a high-quality frame of thoughts. The law of purpose and impact states that if you imitate glad and a success people, you could in the end revel in the same things they do because of the fact you'll begin to sense the same manner and gain the equal results.

How Can Contented Individuals Find Good within the World?

You ought to recognize that pessimistic and not unusual people method conditions in first rate strategies than extraordinary human beings do. The first is that they attention on what they want and then make a concerted try and figure out a manner to accumulate it. Put in a distinct manner, you need to make certain that your goals are clean and which you are confident that you can locate in the crucial attempt to accumulate them, no matter how lengthy it takes.

Second, irrespective of how difficult a situation seems to be, superb people find out the amazing elements in it. It's vital to take into account that errors may be made in some unspecified time in the destiny on your life, and trust me as soon as I say that this is a high-quality thing! There are usually outstanding and terrible elements to each hard circumstance, and it's far as an awful lot as you to determine which direction to take. It is essential that you focus on the immoderate superb.

Make the selection to find out the fantastic factors of some thing in desire to constantly in search of reasons to dislike matters. There is something great in that undertaking, even though it could no longer look like it to you. If you appearance cautiously, you will be conscious it. The reality is, you may experience higher and in addition positive as you look.

It takes mental education to domesticate a exquisite outlook and the notion that you may accomplish any purpose in lifestyles for outstanding wondering to be effective. The reality is that the thoughts is burdened on the way to interest on one element at a time, given enough bandwidth. It's your duty to keep your interest on uplifting mind for a sufficient quantity of time to form neural connections that facilitate the formation of recent conduct.

Just maintain in thoughts that the manner you cope with a tough situation or incident that arises alongside the street is what actually counts. In extraordinary terms, the manner you react will decide how matters flip out. It means that even inside the face of adversity, you have to find out a way to reply undoubtedly. It is viable to counteract bad thoughts by way of way of using growing highbrow repetitions of remarkable affirmations or terms. It's feedback like this as a way to inspire you to undertake an optimistic outlook.

Make The Decision To Be Happy

It is a desire you are making to be content material cloth and lead a satisfied existence.

You have the choice to view topics as half of of full or half of of empty. It's possible that subjects might not usually exercise session. You will come upon hard instances for the duration of your life, however it does not propose you may in no way be capable of have all of it. Nobody can declare to have had a beautifully linear lifestyles. Along the manner in existence, there might be hills, valleys, and mountains. The secret is to pick to rely your benefits one at a time and to understand every season in choice to living on the matters that did now not pass your way.

You will now and again be permit down via the humans to your life, but it does now not advise that they will be awful people or that they despise you. Choose to appearance absolutely everyone's suitable intentions while you gaze upon them. Believe me, the bulk of human beings paintings in fact hard to become their fantastic. Consider all of the tremendous matters they've got finished for you in the past in location of living on the simplest little element they stated which you did now not like.

Ultimately, pick out to be happy irrespective of what takes vicinity. Every condition has a blessing underneath it that is hidden. It's your undertaking to discover it!

Action-Oriented Mentality

If there's one issue lifestyles has taught us all, it is that happiness comes effects at the identical time as matters are going properly. But while unanticipated barriers upward thrust up, our religion is challenged. We display our actual attitudes to ourselves and everybody round us at the same time as we are faced with annoying conditions. Make fantastic the image you provide is one of positivity.

You won't believe how hundreds it'll gain you to select to be fantastic. Your subconscious and aware minds is probably not able to preserve in thoughts any doubts or bad mind at the same time as you count on with any luck. Upon studying the art work of high-quality thinking, your lifestyles will go through an abundance of top notch changes.

Your thoughts will start to characteristic in a nation in which feel-appropriate hormones are flowing freely. It will offer you with the effect that a heavy load has been removed out of your shoulders and which you are all of sudden moderate all yet again. You may additionally experience a vast increase in self assurance and be willing to address hard obligations which might be outside of your comfort region.

Reducing your self-limiting ideals permits you to experience new ranges of boom you in no way can also have belief viable. It's like releasing the brakes in your existence. Put each other way, you may in reality transform your life on the equal time as you operate the energy of extraordinary idea.

Let's have a look at a real-international example of the effectiveness of constructive thinking. A youngster goes outdoor to play together with his buddies. They gather their athletic abilties through on foot. Playing with pals fosters a enjoy of teamwork and improves a infant's communique talents. Their capability to analyze their environment drastically contributes to the improvement of their innovative abilties. Playing with others is a fundamental interest that fosters the improvement of a child right right into a properly-rounded grownup with sensible lifestyles competencies.

In truth, those talents undergo a ways longer than the preliminary feeling that sparked them. Years from now, their athletic skills might possibly assist them get a university athletic scholarship, or their functionality to art work properly in a set environment at the side of talking well could likely assist them succeed as senior coping with accomplice.

This is called the "boom and construct idea," steady with Fredrickson. This is due to the truth, similar to a little one, at the same time as you revel in top emotions, your thoughts can be extra open and your feel of possibilities will broaden. This consequently substantially aids within the development of latest capacity devices that you may locate beneficial inside the destiny.

Our World is Created By Our Thoughts

Examine your environment. What are you capable of see?

The reality is that the whole thing you notice, at the side of chairs and people, have come to be initially generated and visible through a unmarried individual's mind. In another context, a few element your thoughts can be given as actual with and think is surely capable of materializing. Some humans, but, could consider that this is in reality another terrible first-rate questioning tactic which you have heard approximately masses. We had no longer been able to showcase the effectiveness of extraordinary thinking through technology up to date. However, way to quantum physics, we're able to now attain this.

The potential to apply your thoughts to trade reality to suit your factor of view exactly is what quantum physics has decided to us approximately the man or woman of the human thoughts, belief, and perspectives approximately truth.

For instance, an huge amount of research has mounted that particles make up the universe, irrespective of the claims of sure scientists that waves do. They all made the decision to take a seat lower back and advantage a distinct perspective after years of fights. At that issue, they determined that, in accordance with medical predictions, the universe changed into long-established of waves or particles. That is precisely what they may understand inside the event that they had been to don't forget that waves produced the foundation of the universe. And this is precisely what it regarded like, assuming that is how they believed it have become constructed of waves.

Similarly, due to the truth you enjoy that some subjects are out of your control, you maintain believing that truth is what it is. But in truth, matters are the manner they'll be because of the fact you count on them to be. Funny, huh?

This concept also explains why such numerous wealthy individuals offer such weight to the strength in their thoughts and imaginations. People artwork to cultivate their mind-set after growing their reality based mostly on their beliefs. This is in the long run what brings them giant happiness and fulfillment. Then you start to question why the everyday individual holds different humans liable for their mistakes and conditions. The secret is to appearance deeply within for the motives of every achievement and failure.

"If your success in existence is primarily based to your attitude, what are you going to do about it?" is a important question to ask in this situation.

Chapter 2: Advantages Of Maintaining An Upbeat Attitude

It's common to appearance optimism as a unique function that makes life happier and in addition pleasant, and those are not without a doubt words. Positive questioning improves our life in such quite some techniques, consisting of our relationships, self assurance, and not unusual health. These are a number of the reasons you must adopt a excessive nice thoughts-set in case you do now not have one already.

Optimists Handle Pressure More Efficiently

It's common to experience hard instances in life on positive seasons. Still, as compared to a pessimist, only a tremendous logician can deal with the hard state of affairs properly. One observe located that optimists are extra willing to pay attention on what they may do to remedy the present day problem at the same time as faced with a hard situation.

Instead of wallowing in your disappointments and annoyances, you have to make a course of action or ask for assist from people who can provide steerage or assist.

Staying Positive Can Boost Your Immune System

Recent research have demonstrated that the mind has a profound impact at the body. Your frame's immunity is the shape of impacts. According to at least one take a look at, the frame's immune reaction to a flu vaccination is compromised while precise brain regions connected to ugly feelings are inspired.

Furthermore, studies have validated that an positive outlook on a certain problem of your existence, which embody your instructional not unusual overall performance, strengthens your immune tool in contrast to those who view the world negatively.

Actually, retaining a excessive super thoughts-set on life is critical for reinforcing our immunity and supporting us in managing strain, each of which make contributions to our preferred well-being. According to greater research from the Mayo Clinic, having a outstanding outlook extends one's life expectancy and reduces the chance of coronary heart ailment-associated deaths similarly to the probability of melancholy.

It's dubious, though, how wondering surely can also impact our fitness in a scientific manner. However, we also can decorate our popular well-being with the useful resource of gaining knowledge of a manner to manipulate stress greater correctly and abstaining from dangerous conduct.

The Health Benefits of Keeping a Positive Outlook

It has been tested that questioning surely lengthens our lives and improves our feelings in evaluation to thinking negatively. The truth is that our our our bodies reflect each lousy belief we've got in our heads. To placed it every other manner, we have a propensity to worrying up our muscle groups and feature poorer super sleep even as we are aggravating and depressed. We get sad with the entirety and grow to be demanding about the future. But while we attempt to conquer those bad emotions, we save you the physical outcomes they have got on our our our bodies and reclaim our fitness.

A More Resilient You May Achieve It

To be resilient is truely so as to face up to tough conditions. When you technique a difficult occasion with resilience, you very very own the braveness and the energy wished to overcome it. When faced with such instances, you do now not break down; as an alternative, you pick out up the factors and continue to remedy the issue as an entire.

An positive person can be capable of see the massive photograph and perceive opportunities to remedy problems everywhere they rise up. You use your assets and free will to resolve the problem instead of giving up. You flow into above and beyond to invite those on your immediate surroundings for help each time viable.

Positive thinking may be a effective safety inside the path of issues like depression inside the course of a disaster, which encompass a natural catastrophe or a worry assault, in accordance to investigate. This is mainly real for resilient humans. The nicely information is that resilience and advantageous questioning are features that may be developed. You are in a better function to benefit in the short and lengthy phrases at the same time as you domesticate genuine emotions.

The Quality Of Your Relationships With Others Improves

Positive thinking improves your capacity to make an amazing first impact on one-of-a-kind humans. You have to understand that excessive super people usually have a tendency to draw others greater because of the fact they provide the idea that they may be capable of keep friendships going. This have to help to offer an motive for why excellent thinkers generally tend to guide busy social lives. The same holds proper for romance partnerships. As a give up end result, folks that expect and act certainly are much more likely to draw hobby from the other intercourse or equal intercourse than folks that do the alternative.

Sharper And More Concentrated

You can exceptional come to terms with the fact that your trouble is not terrible while you renowned that it's far viable for anyone on your location to have experienced it in the past. That's on the identical time as you discover the manner to hold interest in any difficult situation. And the key is to anticipate really in each condition.

Confidence Boost

Thinking genuinely makes you experience very confident about your skills and skills. In truth, whilst you assume genuinely, you get hold of the amount of your capabilities and keep away from trying to alternate who you are. Put a few special way, you amplify an appreciation and affection for who you are, and this notably boosts your self assure.

They Lead More Fulfilling Lives

Researchers have placed facts that shows folks that anticipate in reality and lead constructive lives typically live longer than those who do no longer. This is because of the truth they end up extra green in life by using way of gaining knowledge of to identify possibilities at the same time as others do not.

You need to preserve in mind the regulation of enchantment, among different matters. Positive thoughts will draw first rate topics into your lifestyles. As a quit end result, domesticate gratitude for the entirety on your life. If you have got a observe the possibilities in your problems rather than that specialize in them, your existence will decorate faster as opposed to later.

Having stated that, you want to recall that questioning absolutely does now not propose making quick decisions in lifestyles. Indeed, research have indicated that optimism can every now and then backfire. It isn't always critical to overlook the awful data in case you want to find the first rate issue. Always try to make the most of tough situations, but base your choices in your talents.

It is a truth that awful topics will continually occur. You will experience sadness and damage from others spherical you sooner or later on your lifestyles. This does now not suggest that you are up closer to the location.

Rather than attempting too tough to hold a grudge, you have to understand that such subjects do appear and approach the trouble realistically. In this manner, matters gets higher for you and you can expand from all your terrible reports.

Determining the Nature of "BLUE" Thoughts

"BLUE" features as a code word.

B- blaming

L- seeking out the awful records

U- sad guessing

E- exaggeratedly horrible

The fact is that the ones mind are too pessimistic to be a few thing other than the truth. You need to be aware of the reality that we count on greater than 70,000 thoughts an afternoon. These thoughts often have a tremendous have an impact on on our emotions and the picks we make in life. Thoughts that have automatically run through your head are beyond your manage, however the manner you react to them is something you could manage.

Mental power is depleted even as you do not forget in self-doubt, worry needlessly approximately property you can not manipulate, and dwell on the terrible topics which have passed off for your lifestyles. Here, it is all about you channeling each awful perception into something accurate. The secret's to intentionally educate your mind to expect in a unique way that allows you to supply a boost on your highbrow abilities.

You emerge as a ways more potent than on the identical time as you may stay on horrible mind all day prolonged at the same time as you pick to take fee of your inner thoughts and idea manner. The more effective you are, the more likely you're to be empathetic, powerful, and open. Put in every other way, while you count on clearly, you begin a high first rate chain response that modifies your conduct and ultimately brings fulfillment and happiness into your existence.

How then are you able to recognize that pessimistic mind?

Blaming Yourself

Yes, every person parents has to certainly be given obligation for our deeds. That's a superb component, however setting too much blame on oneself can backfire. Excessive self-blame has been associated with terrible intellectual health and stepped forward threat of depression, constant with research. So have in thoughts of those moments even as you experience like you are answerable for everything that is going incorrect, and consider to definitely take delivery of duty for your movements without constantly being too harsh on yourself.

Looking For the Bad News

Have you ever skilled a really perfect day wherein the whole thing went according to devise, first-rate to have all of it ruined with the useful resource of using an sudden unsightly event? We've all possibly had those days. The most important query, even though, is: What did you do afterwards? What come to be it that you paid extra interest to?

I'm now not great about you, but I could not prevent thinking about what had lengthy past wrong that day. Even at the same time as we've had more than ten superb events that day, hundreds of us usually will be predisposed to come to be engrossed in a single terrible occasion. But you need to recognize that your thoughts becomes very darkish in case you recognition at the terrible topics all of the time. Simply take a step back currently to have a sensible mind-set at the scenario after realizing that. In this way, you could extend a sensible, nicely-balanced plan of action to stay content material fabric even when subjects skip wrong.

Unhappy Guessing

Nobody is privy to what awaits us the next day, or maybe further into the future. You might be right right right here searching in advance to catastrophe if you have a lot properly in keep for your self inside the destiny. Perhaps you are becoming prepared for a take a look at, or probably you have got a presentation at artwork the following day. You're traumatic inside the decrease again of your mind approximately how you may appear silly or how you'll omit out on possibilities in case you flunk that exam.

You must recognize that whilst you challenge terrible emotions into your future, there can be an extraordinary chance that you can begin acting because of this and in the long run carries the prediction to skip. Every time you are making a guess that makes you feel this way, opportunity the exact opposite. What takes place in case you supply the most exquisite and unforgettable presentation certainly anybody has ever seen? What in case you do properly on the test and gather a long way extra opportunities than you could have ever imagined?

The opportunity that subjects will exercise a ways higher than we count on exists typically. Consider all the benefits your fulfillment will result in instead of concentrating on the drawbacks. That will can help you put up greater attempt and diligence in a few thing which you do, if you want to in the end produce superb effects and success.

Chapter 3: Exaggeratedly Negative

Its type of a downhill spiral whilst you persuade yourself that the complete issue has become a large disaster You are going within the wrong course if you start to inform yourself that your work is a shaggy dog story. It's a reality that negativity has detrimental results. If you usually take delivery of as actual with that you're going to fail, you may in no way achieve success. If you already assume you could not pass the examination, there may be no need in taking it. Your odds of experiencing effective results decrease the extra awful you enjoy.

However, you need to make a conscious try to replace those terrible mind with terrific ones. To do this more correctly, strive placing yourself in a chum's function and considering what you'll recommend they do within the occasion that they have been experiencing what you're proper now. Thus, whilst you trap your self wondering terrible, self-defeating mind, provide you with a clean, concise plan to help you flip your existence round and pass toward a better location.

You'll come to appearance that questioning extra realistically wonderful mind in vicinity of bad ones may be fairly motivating and is step one in building the type of existence you preference. It goes to be fairly hard to modify your wondering in case you are obviously willing inside the route of awful wondering. On the opportunity hand, if you begin making gradual adjustments, your mind will eventually go through notable bodily changes. Put some other manner, you may discover it easy to think actually and your mind will start to view you and your abilties in a distinct way.

The Brain Damage Caused via manner of Negative Thoughts

The human thoughts has changed and advanced over time to come to be more able to making judgments and reacting swiftly to threats to protection. In this sense, the human mind is deceived into wondering that there can be an drawing close danger when a person is harassed, worried, or thinks negatively. The combat-or-flight response is as a cease result added approximately with the intention to deal with the existing hassle or danger.

The human thoughts is pressured out physical to cope with or react fast to unsightly thoughts or threats. In this revel in, terrible mind or emotions purpose the thoughts to react as quick as it might if the character faced an coming near near chance to their protection. The brain abilties on the concept that everything is underneath manipulate and functioning properly even as we assume certainly, that means that no movement is wanted.

The response to bad mind is the opposite of this. But because of the truth horrible concept typically does not pose a risk to life, most human beings select to dismiss it. The most important question here is: What percentage of the forced-out, bad mind, and fears endanger the individual's lifestyles?

According to recent studies on human psychology, strain-introduced on horrible mind are overusing this strong protection mechanism, which in turn weakens the immune machine and increases the chance of contracting the illness. This emphasizes how our our bodies and minds are being harmed thru manner of terrible wondering to a extra quantity than we may additionally apprehend.

The Journal of Clinical Psychology states that annoying and horrible questioning have a huge effect on people's functionality to complete each day chores. In this experience, folks who worry fifty percentage or greater of the time display a huge disruption in their capacity to cope with the tough situations they stumble upon on a each day foundation in evaluation to folks that suppose simply.

As a give up cease end result, an increase in terrible thoughts impairs someone's ability for problem-solving and the self-assure needed to do some crucial jobs. Bad mind intrude with an character's capability to digest statistics and count on honestly while the mind is supplied with hard and complicated responsibilities.

In this experience, the research claims that wondering negatively approximately the problems one is going thru does not help in hassle-solving; as an opportunity, it makes it greater tough for people who acquire this to generate thoughts for fixing issues or realistic solutions. It destroys the self-guarantee and religion that fuel creativity and invention, which characteristic the cornerstones of mindsets centered around problem-solving.

Negative mind have an effect on reminiscence, the thoughts (the thalamus and amygdala), and the hormone system, which modify critical additives of the discourse surrounding hassle-solving, comprehension, and conceptualization. As a surrender result, a assemble-up of awful mind impairs your vision, self confidence, self belief, and bravado to tackle a assignment head-on within the hopes of succeeding.

Removing bad mind is essential to enhancing our brain's average overall performance. You can do that thru training your thoughts to concentrate on opportunities that present themselves continuously and at the great. Positive wondering is a powerful tool.

Connecting Thoughts with Deeds

"Thoughts may additionally come at whim, but movements are curbed with the aid of way of will," states Psychology Today. This announcement highlights the distinctions most of the notions even as simultaneously putting in place a fantastic dating between thoughts and deeds.

Generally speaking, one's mind are not unusual with the resource in their interactions with others, their research of their surroundings, and the expertise they collect. Thoughts are often the unfiltered feelings commonplace with the resource of each other's existence research and worldviews. They also are allowed to anticipate some thing they need, whether or not or not or not it is remarkable or terrible. But actions are precipitated via manner of using will and typically inspired through manner of the way they have an effect on distinctive people in the community, at art work, or at college.

The essential forces within the lower back of your thoughts are generally your belief of your self, your degree of self belief, and your vanity. Quite frequently, these mind can turn out to be deeds. The key to accomplishing your desires in lifestyles is frequently located in the sports you carry out. As a stop result, it is vital to take stock of your emotions approximately your self if you're no longer making improvement inside the course of your desires.

Achieving your desires in life calls for perseverance further to repeated action. Self-definitely nicely well worth has a essential position in identifying one's motivation, tenacity, and internal energy—all of which is probably vital for taking motion in the direction of achievement. This demonstrates the effectiveness of awesome wondering.

It serves due to the truth the cornerstone for encouragement, electricity, and self esteem, all of which is probably critical for allowing a person to advantage their primary goals in life, company, and the place of work. Negative mind, but, appreciably restriction goals. Saying "I can not" to yourself will undermine your self warranty and feel of self confidence. It can even make any essential sports activities you do a high-quality deal a whole lot much less a success, so as to prevent you from challenge your goals.

Thus, even though mind and deeds are excellent, they will be inextricably related. On the only hand, someone's moves regularly have an effect on their mind. In this example, lousy deeds often bring about awful thoughts. On the opportunity hand, a person's final actions are notably delivered approximately with the useful resource of the attitude they select, whether or not it's miles effective or awful.

Strategies for Cultivating an Attitude of Optimism

Retrain Your Subconscious

You may also furthermore learn how to permit bypass of the negativity that has been weighing you down and maintaining you from transferring earlier in a number of one-of-a-type techniques. A element of those incidents occurred at some point of your early years, and your frame and thoughts have carried them approximately for a long time. It's these gadgets which is probably keeping you from records your finest capacity.

The retraining of your unconscious may be completed via many activities, along with neuro-linguistic programming (NLP) and tapping. They are vital in facilitating access to the unconscious thoughts, which allows to extend more self-assured and forceful ideals.

Others have retrained their unconscious minds via hypnosis and meditation. To located it some distinctive way, all you are doing is education your mind to allow flow of all the lousy topics that took place in the past and to update them with new, wonderful opinions at the way to take area within the destiny.

I've decided that speakme and taking note of affirmations is one of the best strategies. Positive statements or thoughts that you choice to maintain actual approximately your self are known as affirmations.

Create a list of ten to 20 affirmations. Then, stand in the front of a mirror, read the affirmations aloud whilst dealing with your self in the reflect every within the morning and at night time time earlier than going to mattress. This is regularly called reflect work, and it's far pretty powerful. Daily practice will reason you to step by step start to receive as authentic with the ones claims, as a way to modify the way you think about yourself.

I strongly recommend you to listen to affirmation tapes while you sleep with a purpose to adjust ingrained thoughts. Your subconscious mind is essentially open at the same time as you sleep, prepared to absorb anything you are giving it.

Such affirmation recordings are to be had on YouTube, or you may record your personal with phrases like "I am succeful of having the whole thing I want," "I am powerful," and "I am worthy."

Repetition is the important thing whilst using those strategies. Your unconscious mind need to be constantly fed until your new ideals have taken the area of your antique ones. It is truely useful to preserve this for now not plenty much less than 21 days until the intended effects are decided.

Chapter 4: Dedicate Regular Time To Your Passions

We find it clean to say that we're too busy with our severa social and expert responsibilities. But we moreover want to carve out time for the subjects we are passionate about out of our annoying schedules. Otherwise, we allow negativity and hopelessness rapid eat us at the same time as we do no longer make time and vicinity for the things we revel in.

The secret's to ensure you take the initiative to uphold the boundaries a good way to allow you to follow your passion. Begin with the beneficial resource of dedicating at least one hour each day, loose from distractions from exclusive commitments. Be happy to say no to distinctive requests even when you have to an brilliant way to cultivate a brilliant outlook.

Make Sure You Take Good Care Of Yourself

Numerous research have demonstrated that, further to how we method sleep and exercising, what we eat and drink has a large effect on our emotional nation. As such, you want to understand of what you located into your frame in case you need to anticipate certainly. You can brief determine viable regions for improvement in this technique.

Consider whether or not you have become the right minerals and vitamins to your body from your weight loss plan and whether or not or not or now not it's far a healthy one. Is there a way to change your weight loss plan to enhance your fitness? Research has confirmed that nutrients deficiencies have an effect on our fitness and were related to depressive and worrying signs and signs.

However, it has also been hooked up that getting inadequate sleep at night time might probable have an impact on our thinking through inadvertently promoting awful mind. Similar responses will come from the highbrow and emotional regions at the same time as you start to take appropriate care of your physical body.

Spread Joy So You Can Experience It

Did that displaying kindness to those round you makes you enjoy proper similarly to making them glad? You can set your self up for achievement through taking a minute to reveal kindness to a person or maybe to a whole stranger you meet on the road. It's what is going to permit you to triumph over pessimistic idea patterns.

Thus, treatment nowadays to growth the addiction of showing compassion to oldsters which is probably maximum in need each time you feel down and hopeless. The awful moments will bypass quick earlier than everything disappears, and in the end it's going to come glaringly.

Embrace Life's Little Pleasures

Encouraging and purposefully that specialize in topics that bring you pleasure and happiness is the high-quality technique to assist your mind learn how to expect without a doubt. Get a pocket book most effective for this purpose, and whilst you wake up each morning, write down at the least five topics that make you satisfied and which you plan to attention on that day.

You need to undergo in thoughts a number of categories that you may interest on while doing this. What form of encounters, for example, make you satisfied? Are there any elements of your environment that inspire you? Are there any characteristics approximately you that provide you with greater self-guarantee and satisfaction? The truth is that with the aid of focusing on the matters that supply you satisfaction, you are certainly fortifying the neurological pathways in your mind which can be related to constructive thinking and a powerful outlook on lifestyles.

Turn Adverse Situations into Advantages

Lastly, you may rewire your mind such that regardless of how tough the events, it will instinctively select out to appearance the fantastic difficulty of factors. You will first need to make a conscious try to push yourself to discover the extraordinary elements of each horrific experience.

For instance, it's far better to don't forget that the universe has some thing better in shop for you at the same time as some thing does no longer turn out the manner you had planned. Instead than identifying to view your self as a failure, pick out to learn from each event.

You additionally want to make every attempt to show your limitations into opportunities. If you in all likelihood did now not get the project, maintain in thoughts how you can beautify for the subsequent time spherical instead of pouting and allowing it get to you. You'll sooner or later have a look at that your thoughts will characteristic this way on its personal without your having to tell it to. To placed it every other way, your thoughts could be scanning your existence for delivered encouraging reviews and ideas.

The Role of Language

The truth that thoughts are normally expressed verbally emphasizes the importance of language in nice wondering. This is in particular actual at the same time as having non-public discussions on topics or problems that someone considers or even brings as masses as themselves.

Thus, one's choice of language has a right away relating fantastic wondering. It is tough to preserve satisfied mind, as an example, while one speaks negatively. As a cease give up end result, using language that is uplifting and useful allows create a basis for splendid thinking.

Positive Language

When conveying the identical idea, English speakers regularly have the choice among growing a powerful or terrible statement. For example, the commands to "arrive on the assembly on time" and "do not arrive late" are same. That being stated, the preceding assertion has a far plenty an awful lot much less lousy which means. This demonstrates how language shapes the binary selection to sound both fantastic or negative, which consequently affects mind.

English gives clients the freedom to pick out the tone of their language further to the attitude and mentality which is probably portrayed as it offers many options for terrible speech to be formed in place of greater splendid dialogue. Business professionals say that using a high-quality language possibility will boom the threat of powerful conversation with the beneficial aid of thirty to forty percentage even as in comparison to the usage of a terrible language model.

The form of mind and inner communicate you have is considerably inspired with the useful aid of the language you select, which need to be remarkable. As a result, using uplifting language will help your correct intellectual snap shots. Encouraging requirements which is probably powerful and upsetting will inspire you to have effective interactions along with your family, coworkers, and friends.

A terrific thoughts-set and thoughts-set, which may be essential for selling development in a number of the worrying conditions you're encountering at work, at domestic, or within the community, are also supported through splendid wondering. Therefore, it indicates that an character's behavior and thoughts are considerably inspired with the useful resource of the language or mind they embody, whether or not or no longer or now not wonderful or horrible, implying that this preference has an impact at the person's mind.

The Brain, Positivity, and Negativity in Language

Words have an impact on the mind and the way it plays, consistent with studies on the connection among an man or woman's word desire and mind characteristic. Selecting great terms like "loving-kindness," "love," and "peace," for instance, can regulate how your mind works through growing frontal lobe activity and stimulating cognitive belief.

In this example, the use of encouraging language for a prolonged quantity of time can motive the thoughts's motivational areas to grow to be active. Your mind-set, mentality, artwork ethic, and standard method to particular activities in existence and at artwork will all tremendously exchange due to this.

On the opposite hand, if you constantly pick out out to talk negatively, you save you the discharge of a few neurochemicals which might be crucial for strain manage. As a quit result, speakme negatively can cause a spike in terrible mind, that can then spark off the concern vicinity of the mind.

Stress-inducing chemical materials are launched into the frame as a result. Consequently, the ones hormones and neurotransmitters intrude with the thoughts's capacity to cause and use correct judgment, impairing the mind's ordinary abilties.

As a stop end result, the language that someone chooses considerably impacts the overall thoughts that they maintain. Good mind feed super words, and vice versa. Furthermore, the mounted order of a hormonal balance within the thoughts that fosters strain, an nice outlook, and the willingness to offer one's all is made feasible with the useful resource of wonderful questioning.

On the alternative hand, horrible wondering drastically impairs thoughts feature, resulting in a depressing, careworn-out, and useless mind-set that lacks enthusiasm and force. There are a few topics that one desires to adopt an super manner to adopt fantastic thinking. The essential functions of remarkable questioning, which might be protected under, spotlight those.

Traits of an Upbeat Mindset

Self-Talk

Most human beings continuously communicate with themselves. The inner conversation often begins offevolved the out of doors one. Hence, the use of upbeat language in outside discourse is indicative of excessive top notch thinking. This is due to the truth our language alternatives in the outside speak have an effect on our internal thoughts inside the equal way that the inner talk impacts the outside alternate. As a prevent cease result, it is crucial to speak certainly while accomplishing outside discussion considering that this may help you set up high-quality idea styles.

Chapter 5: Creating An Emotional Safe Zone

When it comes to supporting human beings in managing unexpected situations in their lives, exquisite thinking is crucial. For example, it is not unusual for someone to reply robotically and negatively even as a few detail sudden takes place to them. This is particularly true whilst someone thinks negatively. Positive wondering, instead, creates a highbrow region wherein it is simple to save you, take some deep breaths, and look for greater statistics in advance than making a snap choice. As a result, adopting a extraordinary thoughts-set permits you to approach conditions and lifestyles's occasions with more poise and thoughtfulness.

Additionally, with the useful resource of the use of this technique, you may be capable of positioned some distance many of the applicable occurrence and your response. Negative thinking frequently outcomes in a blurring of the difference among the incident and the reaction, because of this that the frenzy of subjectivity prevents any logical belief. Positive thinking so lets in a thoughtful response following a radical interest of all of the possible possibilities from various angles.

Good Reactions

An incident can be taken into consideration or perceived in a pleasing or awful mild. Positive wondering, but, permits you to view life's events from a impartial or even a effective attitude. Consequently, you can accumulate responsibility on your detail in making matters higher rather than blaming others.

It additionally aids in your deliberate conversation of optimism and self notion to others as nicely. Good answers additionally make a contribution to the improvement of strong, lengthy-lasting relationships with others, which increase others' motivation, happiness, and optimism. Positive relationships actually have a fantastic effect on one's self belief and revel in of self esteem.

Transform Into a Beneficial Influence

An character's mentality, attitude, or perhaps behavior may be significantly inspired with the resource of terrific questioning. Positive thinkers radiate self guarantee of their own abilties and others' ethical rectitude. Because we frequently imitate the people we spend the maximum time with, this is in particular important. This emphasizes how vital it is to make sure that others who emulate you accomplish that during a way that shows driven conduct, appropriate thinking, and wholesome conduct. The crucial cause right right here is to uplift people rather than depress them.

The Value of Upbeat Language

Positive language emphasizes your abilities in preference on your limitations. Additionally, it emphasizes a compassionate attitude, locations more emphasis on someone's competencies than their obstacles, and commonly goals to attract interest to success in preference to failure.

Spoken language that evokes, motivates, permits, and encourages others to attain their entire capability. Positive language is essential for showcasing private strengths and, in flip, for fostering the self esteem, self-assure, and self-belief which might be important for mission goals and conquering obstacles.

The manner to anticipate actually is to recognition on "what succeeds" in preference to "what fails." This mind-set is consequently "trouble-fixing" because it identifies locations in which you can help, clear up, beautify, restore, or improve the troubles which you are in reality coping with. It will boom the individual's capability to triumph over boundaries, which stimulates the generation of answers, reduces depressing dread, and will increase motivation but difficulty.

The Connection Between Upbeat Mentality and Optimism

In many aspects of life—at home, inside the network, and at paintings—a cheerful outlook is needed. Therefore, that allows you to growth your opportunities of achievement inside the place of work, in relationships, and in connecting to social buildings inside the community, you need to actively pursue the fostering and increase of such an thoughts-set.

Adopting and cultivating a nice thoughts-set are in loads of respects in big aspect depending on awesome wondering. It is critical to recognize that adopting a nice outlook on existence is a deliberate choice that someone makes so that you can specially effect their lifestyles, in region of a few aspect that truly takes location organically. As a end result, adopting a tremendous outlook on lifestyles and a fantastic perception device can also assist domesticate a outstanding thoughts-set.

Reading inspirational and motivational debts of a fulfillment humans is one method to domesticate an prolonged-lasting and green positive outlook. You might be inspired and inspired through the use of this, and it's going to furthermore highlight the instances wherein they made the practical selections that introduced them achievement.

A platform for immoderate remarkable thinking and therefore a fantastic thoughts-set may be created through the use of affirmations, visualizing a hit conditions on your thoughts, and actively stopping poor thoughts from taking root. Additionally, number one a proactive way of life will assist you in averting negativity. Your probability of developing and preserving onto horrible thoughts will significantly decrease if you have a hectic time table.

As a end result, this issue emphasizes the importance of excellent thinking and the way it affects the trouble's attitudes and behaviors. In this manner, questioning simply encourages the growth of tremendous moves which might be marked through power, assure, and helpfulness.

Methods for Cultivating an Upbeat Mindset

Step 1: Keep an Eye on Your Thoughts

Observing your mind is the first step toward education your mind to assume in reality. In reality, the majority of our bad thoughts generally generally have a tendency to ground in the course of precise activities, locations, or moments in our lives. We can be creatures of dependancy, which might offer an explanation for this. For instance, you will likely enjoy tension earlier than any upcoming holiday. Alternatively, you may be involved due to the fact you've got had been given an interview developing. In addition, you will be disenchanted because of a large argument you had alongside side your spouse.

It can be simple to provide you with a solution the on the spot you understand the constantly bothersome lousy mind. For example, if you are confused about a interest interview, you could surely start making prepared early and ask people who've prolonged beyond via comparable interviews for guidance.

Since mind are the supply of all topics, be aware of any poor mind you'll be having and any capability triggers.

Step 2: Check Out These Three Daily Perks

We come into contact with situations and people every single day, a number of which is probably real and a number of that are terrible. As a end end result, you can make bigger the exercise of questioning lower lower back on three proper interactions you had at some point of the day earlier than identifying to move to mattress. It may be getting a modern-day consumer, having your associate take you to appearance the sundown, or having someone purchase you coffee at art work. Small gestures like receiving reward from a friend or coworker, taking walks into an antique acquaintance, putting in new pals, or seeing your children play also can rely. These are greater than loads to provide you happiness.

Step three: Acknowledge Someone

Being thankful is important. Gratitude has been shown to boom optimism and probable prevent coronary coronary heart sickness. Starting a thankfulness pocket book, in which you listing all the things you are thankful for each day, is the first-rate location to start. But I've discovered that expressing gratitude in man or woman in place of in reality on paper makes lifestyles some distance greater massive and profitable.

You can file a few issue right here, together with expressing gratitude to your partner, infant, or your self for all your difficult art work, praising a chum, or talking together at the side of your partner approximately their day. Giving a person a shout-out might also moreover appear strange before everything, however ultimately you'll realize how extremely good it feels.

Step 4: Help Other People

Each day is an possibility for us to help someone in want. Most human beings expect that assisting a person is satisfactory approximately giving them coins. However, assisting others also can take any shape from just assisting a chum installation their art work/task to helping a colleague with invoicing. It may be assisting someone in the kitchen with the cooking or the dishes. It can be defensive the door for a person, searching for a stranger a cup of coffee further to volunteering among others. Just find some element that you could do for a person in recent times. Daily, strive putting a grin on a person's face and watch what positivity that has in your existence.

Step 5: Assemble an Upbeat Support System

You may not be conscious, but emotions can also spread. Imagine entering a happy and thrilled location first-class to discover that everyone is depressed and hopeless. What impact will that have on you following an hour or so of assembly with them?

The fact is, you may sense worse on the same time as you go away that room than at the same time as you entered. Therefore, it's critical which you take note of the human beings with whom you engage and spend the majority of a while. Spending spherical with folks who experience whining and setting blame on others can rapid make you want to do the identical. It best makes experience, then, to surround your self with fantastic function models that inspire you to be a higher friend, lover, giver, and man or woman universal.

Step 6: Take Care of Your Mind and Body

It is apparent from research results that taking proper care of your bodily and mental fitness has an impact for your degree of happiness and contentment in life. Your mind will in the end learn to assume favorably because of this.

For example, your frame tends to create feel-particular chemicals even as you workout continuously and devour healthily, that can improve your temper and everyday perspective on existence. Yoga and meditation are of the terrific techniques to cultivate mindfulness and teach the thoughts to count on honestly.

One of the most vital steps in helping you to stay aware about your thoughts and feelings without continually judging them as appropriate or volatile is education mindfulness. Throughout the day, you can set 3 amazing alarms to help you stay conscious. You virtually stop what you're doing and take a big breath while the buzzer sounds. This makes a large distinction in bringing harmony and optimism all over again into your life.

Step 7: For the Sake of Your Own Inner Healing, Release All Negativity

Finding and letting pass of all of our negative mind is one of the secrets and techniques and strategies to turning into top notch. Don't try to save you them; simply let them skip one at a time. These hurtful beliefs are often the supply of our suffering, and if we're unable to permit pass of those detrimental ideas, we are able to in no manner be able to move ahead in lifestyles. The handiest way we can create a cutting-edge framework of putting ahead ideals that allows you to allow our destiny is if we can spoil free from horrible questioning.

One factor I try to do is find out a quiet vicinity to sit down down for ten minutes even as my head is overflowing with awful mind. Shut your eyes and visualize erasing that detrimental assertion. Repeat this until you enjoy as even though you could allow bypass of it.

Step eight: Schedule In Some Time To Enjoy A Pleasure You Deserve

Speaking is not as smooth as doing. That is, however the fact that, most of the maximum crucial actions you may take to restore positivity on your existence. Find out what you enjoy doing thru first taking a look spherical you. What topics is which you adore the movement—the real deed is beside the component. Reading, developing a music, coaching, gambling sports activities activities

activities, watching films, or cooking are a few examples of this.

Begin by means of using dedicating even an hour a day to concentrating at the subjects you're obsessed with. Set apart some time to have interaction in a genuinely amusing and loving interest. You do not want to miss out on the ones items because of the truth these are a number of the topics that have an impact in your diploma of contentment and satisfaction in existence. When there are the fewest distractions, try and get it every day. You'll speedy see how that shifts your thoughts-set to at the least one that is more advantageous than you ever could possibly have imagined.

Chapter 6: Creating A Bright Future

Overcoming boundaries and disturbing conditions in existence is usually what constitutes improvement in human lifestyles. As a give up end result, that allows you to gather, a person ought to discover solutions to the problems and obstacles that each they and the outside worldwide gift to them. It is important to have interaction with the surroundings, and that is appreciably inspired via the venture's capability to mirror, evaluate the situation, and then find solutions.

The hassle with this technique, even though, is that human beings are vulnerable to taking quick cuts. People usually take in any opportunity—one this is short, much less highly-priced, and easy—in terms of challenge desires. Their potential to remedy issues and assume creatively is also adversely stricken by this.

The essential building block of success in some unspecified time in the future of all degrees of lifestyles is the intentional development of pleasant conduct. Good practices, but, are more than truly following a checklist which you discovered in a e-book. Rather, it consists of fostering and developing effective methods that come glaringly to you and help you advantage your preferred outcomes.

However, due to the sector's unpredictability, volatility, ambiguity, and complexity, growing the right techniques and techniques of wondering to get past obstacles and achieve success is not clean. Increasing manage is not the answer to overcoming existence's unpredictability. Rather, gaining knowledge of agility, brief reading, brief questioning, brief invention, and quick creativity will allow one to comply and modify whenever the unavoidable adjustments and evolutions take place. The following discusses some key elements of systems wondering and fulfillment making plans.

Resolving Errors

In the look for achievement, one often encounters failure. The majority of a achievement humans have encountered severa varieties of failure all through their lives and even as they worked in the direction of their goals. As a stop end end result, there is lots of advantage in looking the ones who've finished fulfillment and converted their lives into fulfillment testimonies.

People who're successful are regularly precisely like us. They've failed hundreds inside the past. The difference is they persevered in perfecting their concepts and gadget until they have been in the long run a achievement.

Applying unique and precise techniques which is probably then cautiously and always accompanied each time is normally how fulfillment is attained. The hassle with this systems wondering approach is that the out of doors international is continuously changing and evolving. This implies that due to the fact unique humans can be dealing with one among a kind dynamics inside the out of doors worldwide, the technique used by one character to obtain success won't be as effective for every different.

But it's miles crucial to understand that our method to tackling and finishing a mission is regularly the most hard. This emphasizes the need of pausing, considering the duties and goals handy, and then choosing the high-quality direction of motion to reach dreams fast. It takes time for human beings to figure out the fine and most green methods to finish the identical undertaking. This emphasizes how vital it's miles to pause and assume carefully before identifying a manner to hold so that you can maximize reward and popular average performance.

Furthermore, it's far important to constantly be looking for techniques to beautify commonplace overall performance, mainly through manner of the use of creativity and innovation. In order to discover the top notch way to finish the task and produce exquisite art work, you ought to check and tweak alongside this device.

Creating a Successful Recipe

The approach someone uses to be successful inside the favored spheres of existence or employer is known as the winning gadget. A a fulfillment technique often begins with great questioning. It is vital to have a tremendous outlook regarding the chosen methodologies and the assignment's goals.

In assessment to poor questioning, which highlights capability troubles and so reduces the enthusiasm needed to be successful, you undertake a thoughts-set that appears to remedy problems, innovate, and build paths to achievement in this way. Positive attitudes and techniques of thinking furthermore have an effect on the ones round them. This will growth the opportunity of achievement via fostering an approach and surroundings that is targeted, pushed, and correct.

Furthermore, a triumphing device is usually centered and precise. This focuses the regions of hobby, it absolutely is vital to enhance invention and creativity and lift fulfillment charges. Completing duties effectively is each other crucial element of achievement. "The right way" encompasses many stuff, which encompass treating others properly, inspiring and motivating others, and locating the coolest in each possibilities and problems. Consequently, thinking in reality contributes to growing a popular environment that encourages and propels success on each a non-public and a set degree.

Getting Your Systems in Place

Creating a customized way for planning, questioning, and developing is crucial to moving you toward your goals. This requires a profound interest and comprehension of oneself in addition to the ability to mildew and mentor oneself in phrases of your outlook on lifestyles. This involves converting the terrible and stressful thoughts and internal talk you have got every day with first-rate ones.

Here, the purpose is to simplify your life as a good buy as possible on the equal time as despite the fact that ensuring that your duties and desires are met. As such, it's miles vital that you allow yourself the steeply-priced of considering how you can accomplish obligations greater correctly. Here are some strategies for developing and retaining a a fulfillment tool.

Getting to Know Your Process and Evaluating It

Before you could attempt to correct your questioning device, it's far essential that you realise it. This lets in you to benefit a whole hold close of your abilties, obstacles, and style of operation One of the maximum essential steps in determining in which you in form into the questioning device is taking the time to get to recognize yourself. Assessing your manner is also crucial. If you are staying up until one in the morning, for example, it is able to recommend that you are not getting enough sleep and are locating it difficult to rouse. Thus, self-evaluation will will will let you recognize the elements that are assisting and selling your fulfillment in addition to those which might be impeding it. The next priorities will boom your possibilities of fulfillment.

Chapter 7: Observing Other People

Examining the artwork of others is vital for growing and forming your non-public idea system further to transferring closer to achievement. Therefore, it is essential to examine from a fulfillment humans, whether or not they are famous or clearly a person you admire for mentoring you. Gain critical insights into their techniques, attitudes, behavior, and mentalities similarly to their perception tactics.

Utilizing what's already available to you which will prevail is perfectly best. Go for it if you could use a person else's brilliant wondering or concept technique to help you attain success. To growth your possibilities of fulfillment, you can furthermore alter what you want to fit your precise necessities and the contemporary out of doors situation.

Anticipating Challenges

The route to achievement is commonly paved with limitations and issues. Consequently, the degree of fulfillment is the capability to overcome some of the ones worrying conditions. Anticipated disturbing situations are often only in detail resolved. This means that anticipating problems makes it easier to plot in advance and give you answers than handling surprising ones.

This emphasizes how important it is to devise ahead for limitations. It's important to cultivate the imaginative and prescient essential to apprehend the medium- to prolonged-term destiny. Determining the results of this form of dynamism is also vital. It places you in a completely strong feature to triumph over the ones barriers.

Apart from the advantages of readiness, this sort of foresight enables you to adjust and modify in a way that now not most effective circumvents the worst effects of trade. Additionally, it captures the ones forces of change and transforms them into an opportunity to function price.

Because exchange is a regular, adaptability and flexibility are great developments. The functionality to keep success is decreased inside the absence of agility. This is a end result of the outside environment's regular change, which forces human beings to modify how they bypass approximately reaching fulfillment. It's additionally critical to live open and honest with your self so you can understand and well known the points at which your technique fails. It's important to keep trying even after failing if you need to create successful strategies and ultimately acquire fulfillment.

Every impediment teaches you a few components. You will begin to view your worrying situations in a greater amazing slight and come to be much less important of your mistakes. I promise that there may be a lesson to be discovered out from every warfare so studies from it and improve upon it the following time.

Chapter 8: Understanding The Impact Of Thoughts

The Mind-Body Connection: How Thoughts Shape Reality:

Have you ever contemplated the huge impact your mind ought to your physical global? The mind-body connection is a great phenomenon that demonstrates the captivating interaction amongst our thoughts, feelings, and physical fitness. This complex link famous that our mind can change our reality in strategies we could not have ever expected.

The lens that we use to look and apprehend the location round us is our mind. They taint our encounters, form our feelings, and force our options. Positivity opens us up to limitless opportunities, resilience, and personal development. On the opportunity hand, a pessimistic mindset might also moreover moreover distort our reality, restricting our opportunities and impeding our improvement. We can form our truth and result in the life we need with the beneficial resource of deliberately deciding on empowering thoughts and redefining our viewpoints.

The anatomy of our brains is likewise impacted through way of using the thoughts-body hyperlink. The neuronal pathways in our brains may be reshaped via manner of our thoughts, which additionally create new connections and rewire the mind. Because of neuroplasticity—the mind's potential for version and exchange—we will have an impact on our thoughts and beliefs, which in flip form our reality. Through cognitive sports activities activities, affirmations, and exceptional wondering, we are able to create new neural connections that sell our fulfillment, happiness, and properly-being. Beyond notion and brain rewiring, the thoughts-body connection additionally affects our physical fitness. Research has indicated that chronic strain, pessimism, and unresolved emotional troubles would possibly materialize as bodily illnesses and issues. However, wondering surely, being aware, and controlling pressure can reinforce the immune device, hasten the restoration way, and enhance popular properly-being. We can realize our capability for lively fitness and energy through fostering a healthful mind-frame dating.

Our mind can carry our wants to pass. According to the regulation of appeal, our beliefs and our interest both increase and emerge as more powerful. We might also harness this modern stress and bring our visions of the life we need to stay to fact thru the use of being clean approximately our targets, envisioning our goals, and coordinating our thoughts and moves. By task aware manifestation strategies, we take at the function of co-creators of our reality, directing occasions and drawing opportunities that healthful our dreams.

We understand the arena spherical us thru filters which are furnished through our ideals. They have an impact on our worldwide thru forming our feelings, mind, and behaviors.

We with the aid of risk construct boundaries that prevent us from transferring forward if we've bad mind about our skills or u.S. Of the us of health. But we can alternate those mind into ones that empower us and promote our well-being if we intentionally have a observe and venture them. We create possibilities for personal development, recovery, and transformation while we supply our ideals into line with our tremendous reality.

The mind-body link serves as a powerful reminder of our innate capacity to steer the sector spherical us. Through knowing the impact of our thoughts, viewpoints, and convictions, we are capable of set out on a life-changing route of self-exploration and improvement. We grow to be aware of our limitless ability as we harness the energy of high great thinking, rewire our brains, address our health, and produce our goals to life. Accept the connection among your thoughts and body and note how your mind create the arena you stay in.

The Scientific Evidence Behind Positive Thinking

It has prolonged been believed that happiness, prosperity, and private development are all in massive component relying on awesome questioning. But is that this notably held perception supported with the aid of way of any scientific proof? Positive thinking seems to have a fascinating scientific basis in step with studies inside the fields of neurology and psychology—clinical evidence of the remodeling capability of excessive quality concept and its profoundly suitable outcomes on our lives.

These are the medical proofs demonstrating the existence-improving homes of terrific thinking and its potential to change humans.

1. Brain Rewiring:

Our brains may be remarkably rewired through excellent thinking. By continuously wondering and feeling positively, we are able to set up new neural connections manner to neuroplasticity, the mind's potential to modify and adapt. Research has indicated that parents who've interaction in outstanding questioning practices, which include journaling approximately gratitude or repeating affirmations, have anatomical changes in their brains. The areas related to resilience, emotional health, and happiness end up greater energetic due to those adjustments. We can develop a more upbeat view of life via rewiring our brains to be extra high extremely good.

2. Enhancing Resilience:

The functionality to triumph over difficulty is called resilience, and it could be bolstered with the use of high extremely good wondering. Studies display screen that optimists generally take a proactive, answer-targeted technique to obstacles, seeing them as probabilities for private improvement. People with an upbeat outlook are higher able to control pressure, get better from disasters more quick, and stay effective even within the face of problem. We might also moreover enhance our resilience and conquer boundaries in life greater outcomes via the usage of education our thoughts to pay attention on the good stuff in life and the possibilities that lie beforehand.

3. Improving Physical Health:

Thinking undoubtedly has a large first-rate effect on our physical health in addition to its highbrow fitness benefits. Research has related emotions of optimism and positivity to decrease infection, strengthened immunity, and better cardiovascular health. Furthermore, the ones who've a wonderful thoughts-set in the direction of lifestyles are much more likely to manual wholesome existence that include frequent exercise, a balanced diet, and advanced pressure manage. Positive questioning is one manner that we're capable of actively improve our standard bodily health.

four. Increasing Success and Performance:

Studies have related first-class wondering to increased success and regular performance in pretty some spheres of lifestyles. Optimistic people frequently aim higher, persevere within the face of problem, and show greater stress and inventiveness. They honestly have a better propensity for taking possibilities and making movements. A pleasant outlook fosters sports activities that result in actual accomplishments and therefore results in a self-satisfying prophecy. Adopting a high-quality mind-set allows us to reach our complete functionality and opens opportunities for improved achievement and success.

Positive wondering's transformative strength is compellingly validated thru the era in the lower back of it. Positive questioning has profound consequences on our lives, rewiring the mind, improving resilience, fostering bodily fitness, and enhancing generic ordinary performance. Through planned cultivation of first-rate questioning, gratitude exercise, and the adoption of an constructive mentality, we are able to unfastened up our inherent ability for private improvement, fulfillment, and achievement.

Why You Should Adopt Positive Thinking

Having a extraordinary outlook ought to make all the distinction in a international full of uncertainty and demanding situations. It's not actually a cliche—exquisite wondering is an powerful method that can alternate your lifestyles. By making the planned preference to look the pleasant factor of things, you could open up a international of blessings with a purpose to enhance your relationships, desired achievement, and well-being. This essay will provide you with sturdy arguments for adopting a first rate outlook and display you the way it could decorate every region of your lifestyles.

1. Better Mental Health:

Thinking definitely has a giant effective impact on your highbrow fitness. Developing an effective outlook teaches your mind to peer the powerful components of each situation. This exchange in angle aids in the cut price of strain, anxiety, and despair. Feel-proper neurotransmitters like serotonin and dopamine are released while we think virtually, improving our mood and provoking delight and happiness. You can boom a resilient and upbeat intellectual nation if you want to permit you to cope with life's boundaries with grace and ease by the usage of adopting high-quality wondering.

2. Improved Relationships:

Having a satisfied outlook may have a profound effect for your relationships whilst you remember that positivity is contagious. People are drawn to nice humans thru the use of nature due to the fact they foster an environment this is upbeat and non violent. Thinking really encourages empathy, compassion, and understanding, which lets in you connect with humans on a deeper stage. You can foster a supportive and inspiring surroundings through way of concentrating at the powerful trends and strengths of others on your place. Your relationships increase as a end result, bringing happiness, contentment, and a sense of community.

3. Enhanced Resilience:

Although life is complete of united statesand downs, adopting a superb outlook gives you the fortitude to triumph over demanding conditions and recover from screw ups. Having an optimistic attitude permits you to appearance obstacles as probabilities for improvement and training. It strengthens your electricity of thoughts, tenacity, and self perception in your functionality to conquer any hardships. When you take delivery of as real with you studied truly, you domesticate a "can-do" mentality that keeps you transferring beforehand regardless of boundaries. Choosing to expect definitely gives you the capacity to triumph over boundaries, expand from setbacks, and live a lifestyles of ordinary development.

4. Elevated Success:

Success in all spheres of life is intimately associated with excessive brilliant thinking. You have a better hazard of succeeding at the same time as you technique jobs and dreams with optimism. Motivating, modern, and hassle-solving mind are fueled through the usage of manner of quality wondering. They provide you with the capacity to be conscious opportunities that others may leave out and bypass proactively to gather your dreams. Furthermore, thinking surely generates a magnetic environment that attracts in nicely matters and hazard meetings. This is how first-class questioning attracts fulfillment. Adopting a super outlook on lifestyles positions you for fulfillment and achievement.

Adopting a awesome outlook on lifestyles can revolutionize all sides of your existence. People who select to undertake a extremely good mentality can benefit from improved relationships, higher resilience, advanced intellectual health, and prolonged success, to name some blessings. You can also moreover unleash a outstanding power inner yourself to influence your fact and design a glad, fulfilled, and functional lifestyles by the usage of coaching your thoughts to concentrate on the exquisite. So, take the threat, adopt an optimistic outlook, and set out on a path of excellent possibilities and private improvement.

Chapter 9: Cultivating A Positive Mindset

Recognizing Limiting Beliefs and Negative Self-Talk:

It's essential to pick out and cast off proscribing thoughts and terrible self-communicate close to non-public improvement and self-improvement. These deeply rooted cognitive strategies can avert our improvement and keep us from information our best ability. We can triumph over those self-imposed constraints and open up a international of opportunities through developing a immoderate notable mind-set.

Below, we can observe the way to emerge as privy to restricting thoughts and horrible self-communicate, in addition to how growing super questioning can also moreover result in achievement and private transformation.

Deeply ingrained views approximately the place and ourselves that restriction our selections and preclude our improvement are known as limiting beliefs. They regularly give up end result from terrible self-perceptions, societal conditioning, or unsightly sports from the beyond. The first step to emancipation is acknowledging the ones mind. Through introspection and the identification of the ideals that restrict us, we are able to confront and reinterpret our thinking. By substituting powerful thoughts for restrictive ones, exceptional wondering permits us to create new opportunities and achieve self-reputation.

The highbrow talk that feeds emotions of inadequacy, complaint, and self-doubt is known as horrific self-communicate. It weakens our shallowness, inhibits our creativity, and makes it more difficult for us to take possibilities. Being conscious of our bad self-speak conduct and actively substituting them with uplifting and supportive ideas are key additives in cultivating tremendous wondering. We can escape the vicious cycle of negativity and increase resilience and self-perception with the aid of embracing a boom attitude, conducting self-compassion physical games, and practising affirmations.

Thinking in reality has a huge effect on our self warranty and feel of self. Positive questioning fosters a robust enjoy of self confidence and self-perception in oneself. It permits us to look ourselves from the angle of appreciation and reputation of who we're. A wholesome sense of self confidence is fostered via way of wonderful questioning, which lets in us to actually take delivery of our accomplishments, embody our abilties, and face limitations head-on with hope and self assurance. Positive notion patterns help us understand our complete capability and take fee of our achievements.

Embracing the energy of capability is the important trouble to growing an powerful outlook. It allows us dream of a destiny complete of growth and abundance, to appearance opportunities wherein others apprehend limitations, and to find out answers inside the face of issues. We can recognition on opportunities in preference to constraints and traumatic situations in area of solutions even as we adopt a immoderate best mind-set. This highbrow adjustment lets in us to stand life with resilience, openness, and interest, which opens the door to each career and personal development.

Reframing And Challenging Limiting Beliefs

It is an empowering approach that requires self-mirrored image, intentionality, and persistent try to task and reframe limiting thoughts. The following are possible movements you could do to refute and query your proscribing ideals:

1. Determine Your Limiting Beliefs:

To start, pick out out the beliefs that prevent you from transferring ahead. Keep a watch consistent out for horrible self-talk patterns, self-doubt, and areas for your life in that you revel in unfulfilled or unmoving. Exploring your mind and feelings in a magazine can also help you see reoccurring situation subjects or mind which may be limiting your ability.

2. Question the Evidence:

After figuring out a proscribing notion, test the statistics that lends credence to it to refute it. Consider whether or not your concept is supported thru objective proof or if it is only a prevent result of your preconceptions, fears, or studies in the past. Search for counterexamples and opposing viewpoints to the belief. You come to appearance that your limiting idea might not be as actual or robust as it first seems through this device.

three. Actively look for proof to refute your limiting belief to find out supporting evidence. Seek for instances of successful humans in the fields you experience you are not top notch at. Look for anecdotes, endorsements, or examples of humans who've defied your perception or conquered comparable barriers. This may additionally moreover astonish you and offer evidence that assessments and broadens your worldview.

four. After you've got got burdened the veracity of your proscribing notion, exchange it to a greater empowering and sensible belief. Write a reassuring and upbeat message that refutes the traditional interest and allows the supposed end result. Replace your limiting mind-set, "I'm no longer excellent sufficient," as an example, with something greater great, like "I am continuously developing and analyzing, and I absolutely have unique strengths to provide."

five. Practice Affirmations and Visualization: Use empowering affirmations and visualization to reaffirm your new beliefs regularly. Every day, preferably inside the the front of a mirror, repeat your reframed notion and photo yourself dwelling as loads as it. To make those techniques extra a achievement, use your senses and your emotions. These strategies help in progressively rewiring your mind to enhance your new, empowered mind.

6. Take Action: Move out of doors of your comfort region in tiny, possible moves to confront your proscribing ideals. By

conducting what you as quick as believed modified into no longer feasible, you disprove your antique perspective and provide proof on your new, effective conviction. Enjoy your victories and make use of them to spur your self immediately to keep pushing over your limitations.

7. Encircle Yourself with Support: Look for a community of friends, mentors, or coaches who can offer aid, duty, and route. You can depend on their useful resource inside the direction of times of self-doubt or unhappiness as you proportion with them your course of questioning and reframing your restricting beliefs. Their viewpoints and mind can assist you in preserving motivation and gaining sparkling views.

Note that it takes time to confront and reinterpret proscribing beliefs. Celebrate every little step you're taking in adopting empowered attitudes, be type to your self, and characteristic patience. You may additionally moreover exchange your mind-set and realise your complete functionality with perseverance and willpower.

Overcoming Self-Doubt And Fear

Fear and self-doubt can act as bold obstacles within the manner of achieving our dreams. They undermine our self perception, murmur doubts in our ears, and prevent us from making the essential improvement inside the path of our goals. Nonetheless, we are in a role to overcome worry and self-doubt with the beneficial useful resource of using the strength of powerful thinking, and we may also recognize our desires with unflinching notion and commitment. We discuss the reworking energy of extremely good thinking and the manner it is able to help us triumph over fear and self-doubt. We moreover provide workable strategies for using splendid thinking to actualize our aspirations.

1. Rewiring Your Attitude:

Overcoming self-doubt and rewiring your mind-set are by way of and huge facilitated with the useful resource of first-rate wondering. You can confront the terrible ideals which might be preventing you from transferring beforehand and trade your viewpoint with the useful resource of deliberately deciding on to assume definitely. Put self-notion and affirmations that bolster your abilities and abilties in place of self-doubt. Positive mind assemble a highbrow environment that helps resilience, self warranty, and an unwavering perception in your functionality to actualize your goals. This occurs when you feed your mind with tremendous mind regularly.

2. Adopting a Growth thoughts-set:

Overcoming fear and self-doubt calls for a increase thoughts-set. Accept the concept that with dedication and difficult art work, you may enhance your talents, intelligence, and competencies. Recognize that barriers and setbacks aren't symptoms of failure, but as a substitute chances for development and getting to know. A boom mentality is fueled by way of the use of super wondering, which makes it possible to view setbacks as short diversions, hurdles as stepping stones, and failures as stepping stones to victory. When you adopt a increase attitude, you boom resilience and resolution and conquer fear and self-doubt to attain your dreams.

3. Cultivating Affirmations and Visualization:

These strategies are effective manner of bringing your goals to existence. Lean at the power of high-quality thinking to look yourself mission your desires in colourful detail. Make a intellectual photo of the life you need, entire with the emotions, images, and noises that encompass success. Imagine your self residing your dream, attaining milestones, and overcoming barriers with self perception. Use affirmations to enhance your visualization method. Affirmations are uplifting feedback that reaffirm your self esteem and capability to realise your desires. Daily repetition of those affirmations will permit you to internalize them and retrain your unconscious to guide your desires.

4. Taking Inspired Action:

Intentional movement should manual first-rate idea; it's miles insufficient to depend most effective on fine questioning. Make a plan to keep and destroy down your dreams into manageable chunks. Establish modest, realistic desires on the begin to benefit momentum and self perception. No count extensive range how tiny a step you're taking, it builds your notion to your electricity to actualize your desires and allows your exceptional outlook. Knowing that fulfillment and increase are genuinely across the nook, embody ache and confront your anxieties. Your desires can turn out to be a reality through manner of using remarkable wondering to encourage you to take inspired motion.

five. Embracing a Positive Environment:

The people you partner with have a massive impact to your outlook and ability to face tension and self-doubt. Be inside the employer of upbeat, encouraging folks that encourage and uplift you. Look for coaches, mentors, or like-minded people who've done what you want in life. Their help, path, and existence instructions can pork up your optimistic outlook, provide insightful recommendation, and make overcoming obstacles less complicated. Building a strong assist gadget permits you get hold of as actual with more for your desires and your self.

Leveraging exquisite thinking is the first step within the effective adventure of conquering fear and self-doubt. You can also appear your aspirations with unshakeable perception and persistence with the aid of rewiring your thoughts, adopting a increase thoughts-set, carrying out visualization and affirmation practices, appearing on idea, and surrounding your self with high-quality humans. Never overlook about that your mind can change your lifestyles. Accept optimistic wondering, conquer fear and self-doubt, and test as your desires come real. When you have got faith for your abilties and the efficacy of superb wondering, the opportunities are infinite.

Embracing Positive Affirmations

An powerful technique for changing your mindset and assisting you in understanding your goals is using fine affirmations. Through the use of first rate thinking and planned confirmation of your goals, you could domesticate an inner surroundings that allows self-self guarantee, adaptability, and unwavering resolve.

Positive affirmations are declarations that constitute your first-class situation or cease end result. They are purposefully designed to recognition your interest, bolster immoderate exceptional thoughts, and synchronize your subconscious thoughts along with your goals. Affirmations can exchange the way you suspect, enhance the way you spot your self, and offer you with greater self notion. You might also additionally furthermore appeal to possibilities and boost up the tool of manifesting your aspirations thru over and over repeating terrific affirmations.

Your affirmations might be greater effective if they may be present worrying, specific, and private. Affirmations should be framed as despite the fact that they already exist. Be particular about what you want to occur. Say, "I am a success in all areas of my life," as an instance, in choice to, "I can be a fulfillment." Allow your affirmations to arouse effective emotions and a revel in of alignment in you thru the use of aligning them collectively with your middle ideals and dreams.

For affirmations to be effective, consistency is crucial. Repeat your affirmations every day, preferably within the morning or right in advance than mattress whilst your mind is open to receiving them. Repetition rewires your unconscious wondering and serves to enhance favorable attitudes. Accept the repetition technique as a threat to useful resource your effective outlook and domesticate a strong feeling of self-perception.

Use all your senses when chanting affirmations to increase their overall performance. Imagine your self dwelling the life of your goals, revel in the emotions that include accomplishing your desires, and photo the elements of interest, sounds, and sensations that include success. By the use of all of your senses, you may create a wealthy and captivating revel in that allows your subconscious thoughts to firmly hold your affirmations.

In attempting instances, affirmations can act as robust slings. When faced with disturbing situations or self-doubt, firmly repeat your affirmations. Make use of them as a constant reminder of your innate potential, fortitude, and functionality to overcome any hassle. Affirmations resource you in preserving an advantageous outlook by way of the use of substituting steadfast faith in your self and your goals for uncertainty and fear.

Although affirmations are an effective tool, deliberate motion must moreover examine. Affirmations can function a guide for intention-placing and scary movement in the direction of understanding your desires. Divide your desires into manageable sports sports and make a regular attempt to perform them. Sync your terms, deeds, and mind with the uplifting affirmations you repeat to create a effective strain that actions you in advance.

Thank the universe for each breakthrough you take in your quest. Recognize the effect of remarkable wondering to your lifestyles and have a laugh even the little victories and achievements. You can also furthermore entice extra reasons to be thankful and enhance happy emotions by means of the usage of way of working in the direction of celebration and thankfulness.

Adopting amazing affirmations is a existence-converting method that offers you the capacity to convey your aspirations to truth. You can rewire your questioning, growth your self-perception, and synchronize your subconscious mind together along with your goals with the resource of deliberately mentioning your needs. You can use the electricity of brilliant wondering to attract possibilities and recognise your dreams with the aid of the usage of manner of the use of affirmations constantly, and again and again, and integrating them into your each day life. Accept the electricity that exists inner you, create empowering affirmations, and watch as your right thoughts produce wonderful consequences.

Chapter 10: The Power Of Gratitude

The Importance of Gratitude:

Gratitude is a powerful power which could adjust our lives for the better and result in transformation. Combining thankfulness with the energy of excessive extraordinary questioning can help us actualize our dreams and assemble happy, rich lifestyles.

Gratitude is a powerful filter that we are able to use to see the sector. It motives us to refocus our interest from what's missing to what's already there, from problems to opportunities. Gratitude opens our eyes to the abundance all round us and allow us respect the benefits in our lives. When we adopt an attitude of appreciation and possibilities rather than being engulfed via negativity, this perspective shift creates the possibility for excessive fine trade.

Gratitude Practices

We may additionally harness the power of amazing concept and produce our thoughts to lifestyles by the usage of education appreciation. By deliberately expressing gratitude for what we have in our lives, we alternate our vibration, draw prosperity, and domesticate an surroundings that facilitates the boom of our aspirations.

The course to a glad and fulfilled existence is gratitude. It is a way of thinking that permits us to look and price the goodness, no matter how tiny, that permeates each problem of our lives. By accepting thankfulness, we trade our perspective from taken into consideration in reality one among lack to taken into consideration one among loads, of negativity to optimism. Because it connects our thoughts and emotions with the first rate power had to trap and create the existence we preference, this intellectual shift opens the way to manifesting our desires.

1. Gratitude Journaling:

Maintaining a gratitude pocket book is one of the most effective gratitude carrying activities. Every day, set apart some time to don't forget and list the subjects for which you are thankful. Give specific descriptions and find out the feelings connected to every get right of entry to. As a adorable reminder of the richness we have already drawn, this workout not exceptional assists us in keeping our hobby on the great things in our lives. Frequently going back over your thankfulness notebook allows you realize more of your dreams and strengthens the effectiveness of terrific questioning.

2. Rituals of Gratitude:

To solidify the exercise for your life, include each day rituals of thankfulness. Before getting out of bed in the morning, make 3 lists of factors for which you are happy, or make a list of factors for that you are thankful on the stop of the day. Additionally, you'll in all likelihood establish rituals of thankfulness spherical food, pausing to renowned the folks who helped prepare your food in addition to the nourishment you are ingesting. Gratitude becomes ingrained to your each day sports and will become a part of who you're, allowing you to expect undoubtedly and create your dreams outcomes.

three. Acts of compassion:

Gratitude is extra powerful at the same time as it's far expressed thru deeds of compassion. Spend some time being kind to unique people. It might be as smooth as lending a sympathetic ear, providing help, or helping someone who is in need. By expressing thanks to others, you now not best inspire them but furthermore prompt a extraordinary strength chain response that multiplies again to you. Generosity fosters an mind-set of plenty and attracts in extra reasons to be thankful.

4. Gratitude at Difficult Times:

Genuine gratitude is most obvious on the identical time as confronted with hardship; it isn't always restricted to happy instances. When faced with barriers, intentionally look for the benefits and commands they include.

Accept thankfulness as a method for reinterpreting worrying situations and figuring out colorful spots. By adopting a completely unique point of view and working closer to thankfulness even in trying occasions, you expand resilience, improve your notable thinking, and make yourself extra receptive to possibilities for personal development.

5. Gratitude need to be included into your visualization and confirmation techniques. Thank God that your aspirations have come actual and photograph your self living your high-quality existence. Envision the specifics, emotions, and encounters linked to your aspirations as despite the fact that they've materialized. Add affirmations to the ones visualizations that specific thankfulness for your dreams coming proper. Gratitude, affirmations, and imagery artwork collectively to generate a strong lively alignment that accelerates the manifestation approach.

Gratitude As A Catalyst For Manifestation

Being grateful has the power to convert us and help us obtain our goals. When paired with the efficaciousness of first-rate idea, it transforms proper right into a stimulant that releases our opportunities and attracts prosperity into our existence.

Being clearly appreciative and aware about the people, matters, and events in our lives is what it manner to be thankful. We change our attitude from one in all shortage to 1 in every of lots, from pessimism to optimism, whilst we exercise thankfulness. This highbrow adjustment aligns us with the vibratory frequency wished for manifestation, unleashing a torrent of accurate strength. Gratitude draws in what we want and could boom our capacity to make our dreams come authentic. It works like a magnet.

Make running toward thankfulness a each day addiction to completely advantage from its strength. Allocate a sure period every day to undergo in mind and express your thankfulness for all of existence's blessings.

Every day, list 3 things for that you are grateful for your gratitude diary. By working closer to this often, you rewire your mind to pay attention on the high great additives of your existence, which opens up new channels for manifestation. Being thankful maintains us rooted within the right right here and now, allowing us to thoroughly enjoy the opinions which are being furnished to us. Through training mindfulness and being gift, we will understand the possibilities and coincidences which might be crucial to the belief of our aspirations. By connecting our mind and feelings with positivity and appreciating the cutting-edge 2d, we trap greater reasons to be grateful and quicken the technique of manifestation.

Being grateful allows us to exchange our perspective from truely one in each of looking for to at least one in every of already having. Through the exercising of expressing gratitude for our desires as despite the truth that they have already come actual, we're capable of prompt the Law of Attraction.

Incorporate a robust feel of appreciation into your images of your self already pleasing your dreams. Accept and permit seep into your being the feelings and research associated with understanding your goals. This profound alternate of angle we could the universe realise which you're prepared to acquire and bring about the belongings you need to your lifestyles.

Being grateful will boom the strength we supply out and draws extra of the topics we rate into our lives. Our vibratory frequency rises even as we exude appreciation, drawing prosperity and appropriate critiques to us. In addition to helping our manifestation efforts, this high quality strength additionally has an impact at the human beings and conditions in our instantaneous region, spreading optimism and starting up doors to new possibilities.

Though gratitude is a effective manifesting reason, it have to be combined with stimulated movement. While gratitude lets in to deliver our mind and feelings into concord, it's miles our planned, harmonious acts that assist us apprehend our dreams. With the gratitude-cultivated actual thoughts and strength guiding you, take inspired movement inside the route of your goals. Have faith inside the process and maintain your eyes open for any omens or coincidences that might present themselves.

Gratitude fuels the strength of immoderate brilliant notion and aligns us with the riches we desire, making it a effective catalyst for manifestation. We can also additionally construct a powerful synergy that allows us understand our desires with the useful resource of growing an attitude of gratitude, appreciating the modern-day-day moment, changing our perspective, and appearing inspired. Adopt a mind-set of thankfulness, and be conscious how the universe works in your gain to realise your goals with boundless possibilities and eternal optimism.

Chapter 11: Cultivating Optimism Finding The Silver Lining

The Role of Optimism in Manifestation:

Optimism is the important trouble to unlocking our aspirations and dreams. It is a beacon of optimism in an unsure international. It is a stress that actions us ahead, giving us the potential to move beyond worrying situations, capture opportunities, and apprehend our best goals.

Being high pleasant is greater than handiest a passing feeling; it is a sensible manner of questioning and a planned selection to appearance the extreme aspect of factors and all the possibilities in existence. It consists of fostering an positive outlook and the feeling that barriers are certainly transient issues in preference to insurmountable limitations. Being positive offers us the ability to face the manifestation technique with fortitude, unshakable religion, and an unrelenting strength of will to our dreams.

Optimism's Place in Manifestation: 1. . Vibrational Alignment:

Optimism makes our beliefs and goals vibrate in unison, bringing our thoughts, emotions, and behaviors into concord with the frequency of our goals. When we method manifestation with a great outlook, we release a remarkable power that draws property and opportunities into our lives, getting us in the path of our supposed cease end result.

2. . Adaptability in the Face of Difficulties:

Manifestation journeys regularly consist of obstacles and disappointments. Optimism gives us the fortitude required to overcome these boundaries. It lets in us to see stressful conditions as opportunities for development and training in location of as justifications for giving up. Keeping an advantageous outlook allows us to discover our inner electricity, adjust our techniques, and keep going until our dreams come real.

3. Increasing Intention and Focus:

Having optimism lets in us be more intentional and laser-centered on our desires. Our thoughts turn out to be laser-focused on attracting and manifesting our desires at the same time as we remember in our capability to obtain them. By aligning our subconscious thoughts with our aware intentions, this multiplied hobby improves the precision and readability of our manifestation manner.

four. Activating the Law of Attraction:

his effective everyday principle asserts that what's like draws like. Optimism draws specific subjects, coincidences, and people who're encouraging into our lives like a magnetic strain. We can generate an energy resonance that draws the precise conditions and possibilities needed to convey our aspirations to existence by means of running closer to optimism.

Optimism is the gas that makes topics take place; it offers our path steadfast faith, courage, and strength. By harnessing the energy of top notch wondering, we also can higher align our desires and draw in the plethora of opportunities that lie earlier of us by means of the usage of manner of directing our mind, emotions, and behaviors closer to our desires.

Strategies To Foster Optimism Optimism proves to be a crucial driving issue inside the pursuit of our goals, assisting us get beyond stressful conditions and understand our satisfactory aspirations. This manner of questioning gives us the ability to appearance the satisfactory in the complete factor, enlarge resilience, and use amazing wondering's transformational electricity.

Using the ones possible techniques, you may enhance positivity, domesticate optimism, and firmly accept as proper with in your dreams.

1. Develop Self-Awareness:

Optimism is fostered while self-awareness is gift. Spend some time watching your feelings, thoughts, and responses to diverse activities. Determine whether or not or no longer self-limiting thoughts or terrible belief conduct are impeding your optimism. Once you are aware of the ones styles, you could intentionally confront and reinterpret them, swapping them out for empowering mind and convictions which might be regular collectively in conjunction with your desires.

2. Practice Gratitude: Developing gratitude is a powerful way to foster positivity. Express gratitude on your life's advantages, possibilities, and improvements often. Keep a gratitude pocket e book or make gratitude physical games a part of your ordinary ordinary. Recognizing the wealth you've got already were given on your existence lets in you cognizance at the powerful and creates an optimistic mind-set that attracts in extra motives to be thankful.

3. Remain Positive: Our mentality is regularly inspired by way of using the use of the people we spend time with. It is uplifting and scary to be among splendid, encouraging people. Join masterminds, agencies, and agencies that guide your goals. Look for role models and mentors who percent your goals of fulfillment and positivity. Embracing a top notch environment fosters a putting this is conducive to optimism.

four. Adopt a increase attitude: Optimism can only be more potent via the usage of cultivating a boom mindset. Accept obstacles not as insurmountable limitations, but as possibilities for improvement and training. Celebrate each minor victory you have got along the way, and emphasize improvement in preference to perfection. Optimism and resilience are fueled via a boom attitude, which sees obstacles as possibilities for success.

5. Being remarkable is a call to motion in vicinity of a passive temper. Divide your

aspirations into possible movements and decide to usually acting to your concept. Your self warranty for your functionality to gain your desires grows with each little step you are taking. When your conduct is consistent along with your effective outlook, you construct momentum and take opportunities so that you can assist your aspirations come real.

Chapter 12: Setting Clear And Inspiring Goals

Define Your Dreams:

Every one folks harbors a universe of unfulfilled hopes and aspirations. Determining our actual goals is the first step in the system of making those dreams come genuine. We can begin the techniques at the manner to cause the perception of our aspirations and needs thru surely describing them and using the electricity of brilliant questioning.

Here's a manner to outline your aspirations and dreams in a transforming manner and the way wondering certainly can assist them come right.

1. Starting a course of self-reflected photograph and introspection is a superb location to begin. Consider your values, hobbies, desires, and innermost emotions carefully. What's happy for you? What looks like fireside on your soul? Discover the desires and aspirations that align together with your actual self by using the use of going deeply

into your heart. Your capability to define your desires is primarily based absolutely in this method of self-discovery.

2. Close your eyes and picture your exceptional future in colourful detail. Visualize Your Perfect Future. How does it seem? What is the feeling? Try to visualise the lifestyles you need through using all of your senses. Regularly immerse yourself in this vision, permitting it to paintings like a robust magnet, drawing you in the course of your aspirations. By setting your perfect destiny in your mind's eye, you could recognition your purpose and trap the fantastic energy required for manifestation.

3. Establish Specific and Measurable

Objectives: After you've got were given a easy concept of your goals, divide them into dreams which may be every particular and quantifiable. Give them a concrete, to be had shape. Establish the checkpoints so one can imply your development at every diploma. Establishing goals permits you stay centered on the route to manifestation and creates a street map for your efforts. Recall that being particular gives your thoughts the ability to visualize and draw inside the opportunities and property you want.

four. Create affirmations that are fantastic and supportive of making your aspirations come actual. These are affirmations of your strength that unique your goals and reaffirm your faith in their popularity. Internalize the first-rate message of these affirmations thru repeating them each day. Your unconscious mind may be reprogrammed to line up with the electricity required to attract and appear your desires through way of regularly putting forward your goals.

five. Develop a Positive mind-set: A amazing attitude is vital whilst defining your desires. Accept self-perception, thankfulness, and positivity. Put self-empowerment and positivity in place of self-doubt and negativity. Whether it is thru uplifting groups, podcasts, or novels, surround yourself with high-quality affects. You can cultivate a pleasant mentality an outstanding way to facilitate the belief of your aspirations.

6. Take added about Action: Thoughtful mirrored image is inadequate on its very personal; stimulated motion is needed. Decide what actions you need to take to understand your goals, and decide to continual, intentional motion. Every step you're taking towards wearing out your dreams will growth yourself assure in doing so. Keep an open mind, receive as genuine with for your intestine, and maintain your composure inside the face of trouble. Never forget about that taking movement is what makes your aspirations come real.

The first degree within the reworking way of manifestation is to define your desires and aspirations. You can also unleash the power of incredible wondering to create your exceptional goals with the useful aid of education self-pondered photo, imagining your nice destiny, making precise desires, keeping your dreams, growing a excessive high-quality mentality, and appearing on concept. Accept this as a non-forestall manner and nurture your desires with unshakeable conviction, readability, and remedy. Watch in wonder as your dreams come actual correctly as you supply your dreams, thoughts, and deeds into alignment. This will exchange your existence in approaches you in no way may want to have imagined.

Creating SMART Goals

When we make deliberate plans and move in the direction of them, desires come real. Setting SMART desires is essential to ultimate the success hole among aspiration and fact. These targets provide a path, bringing our optimistic thinking and deliberate pastime into concord and advancing us in the path of the conclusion of our goals.

1. Comprehending SMART dreams:

The phrases "unique, measurable, capacity, relevant, and time-sure" are abbreviated as "SMART." Every element of a SMART purpose gives our dreams a further diploma of precision, responsibility, and clarity.

Particular: A well-defined and unambiguous SMART aim. It responds to the following queries: Specifically, what do you choice to carry out? What is the preferred effect or final results?

Measurable: A SMART goal may be measured. It has requirements or markers to song improvement and grow to be aware of whilst the aim has been met.

Realistic and feasible given your instances, skills, and to be had property, a SMART goal is on hand. It assessments your limits with out becoming an excessive amount of.

Relevant: A SMART purpose enhances your overarching dreams and aspirations. It is vast and pertinent to every your dream attention and your non-public improvement.

Time-positive: A SMART motive is connected to a cut-off date or time restrict. It maintains you inspired and engaged while instilling a experience of urgency.

2. How to Set SMART Goals:

a. Consider Your Dreams: Get began out thru the use of wondering once more in your aspirations. What specific end result or accomplishment would possibly help you get in the direction of your aim? Clearly u.S. What you want to advantage.

b. Make it Specific: Condense your dreams right into a easy reason. What, wherein, even as, who, and why need to be described. Clearly define your desires, and be as particular as viable.

c. Include Measurable Criteria:

Choose symptoms or requirements to gauge your achievement and development. Decide how you can realise you've got completed your goal. It can be a monetary purpose, an success, or a particular cease end result.

d. Make Sure It's Doable: Evaluate the viability of your objective. Think approximately your to be had device, capabilities, and constraints. Make great it pushes you however is feasible with sufficient artwork and determination.

e. Align with Relevance: Consider how your motive relates in your broader vision and desires. Make effective it indicates your values and passions and fosters your personal improvement.

f. Establish a time body: Give your aim a completely unique timeline or lessen-off date. This offers you a sense of urgency and keeps your reputation. If required, divide your intention into more possible benchmarks.

g. Review and Improve: Evaluate your SMART objectives often and make any corrections. Recalibrate your moves to stay on route, and understand your accomplishments alongside the manner.

3. Using Positive Thought:

Make extraordinary wondering the inducement in the back of your SMART objectives. Develop a effective outlook and reaffirm which you recall you can accomplish your objectives. Envision the a achievement end result and allow yourself feel all the proper feelings that include it. Allow your movements to be driven by way of manner of affirmations and positive thoughts, and draw in the possibilities and assets you need.

The Power Of Goal Visualization

Visualization is a powerful device that facilitates us be a part of our mind with our goals and unharness the energy of our imagination. When coupled with constructive thinking, it acts as a trigger for our aspirations to return real. The approach of truly envisioning and experiencing our favored consequences, referred to as purpose visualization, ignites a strong pressure that movements us inside the route of understanding them.

The Science of Neuroplasticity and the Mind-Body Connection:

Visualization draws on those scientific fields. Our brains apprehend shiny intellectual pictures of our desires as actual activities, firing the identical neural circuits as even though we have been experiencing them. Through this manner, our unconscious thoughts is inspired, aligning our desires and strengthening our self guarantee that they'll be potential. We can use aim visualization to manipulate the way our mind create our reality.

How to Use Goal Visualization in Practice:

a. Establish a Calm Space: Look for a peaceful placing in which you can pay interest with out interruptions. It is probably a park, a motel, or some other place that allows you experience balanced and comfortable.

b. De-pressure and middle your self: Breathe deeply a few instances to assist your body and thoughts lighten up. Let cross of all your troubles and anxieties so you can turn out to be emotionally and mentally open.

c. Visualize Clearly and Detailedly: Shut your eyes and picture your self accomplishing your selected very last effects. Use every sense to colour a smooth intellectual photo. Immerse your self in the emotions associated to your achievement through seeing the colours, being attentive to the noises, and feeling the textures.

d. Involve Your Emotions: As you photograph your motive, revel in the good emotions that rise up. As even though you had been residing out your desires proper now, revel in the happiness, contentment, and delight. Accept those feelings and allow them to boost your conviction that your goals will come to skip.

e. Make Visualization a Regular Practice thru Being Consistent and Repeating. Allocate a selected duration each day to engage within the visualization system. The vision strengthens your perception and draws the favored opportunities and assets to you as you repeat it time and again until it receives deeply embedded for your subconscious.

Enhancing Visualization with Positive Thoughts:

a. Affirmation and Self-Talk: Pair visualization with strong self-speak and top notch affirmations. Repeat wonderful affirmations that improve your perception that your desires will come to pass as you visualize them. Self-empowering mind and affirmations which might be in step with your desires need to take the vicinity of self-doubt.

b. Gratitude and Appreciation: Incorporate the ones emotions into your visualization physical sports. Thank your self for the steps you have got already taken and for the future accomplishment of your objectives. By attracting more reasons to be thankful and strengthening the manifestation machine, cultivating thankfulness will increase the strength of advantageous wondering.

c. Overcoming Limiting Ideas:

Visualization and outstanding concept methods assist you in recognizing and getting over proscribing thoughts that might be impeding your development. As you visualize your goals in exceptional detail, look at any doubts or horrible thoughts that floor. Question and reinterpret the ones beliefs, substituting them with empowered, upbeat thoughts that resource your imaginative and prescient.

Using motive visualization, you may use the transforming power of exquisite wondering to supply your wants to lifestyles. You can also deliver your mind, feelings, and beliefs into alignment with the reality you need to create by means of the use of in reality seeing and experiencing your chosen outcomes. When visualization is used continuously, sincerely, and with a powerful mind-set, it is able to become an effective tool for drawing in the opportunities, belongings, and synchronicities you want to make your dreams come actual. Accept the electricity of reason visualization as a ordinary exercise, and take a look at in amazement as your dreams come proper with extremely good ease.

Enhancing Visualization With Meditation

Transformative in nature, meditation fosters readability, mindfulness, and inner serenity. It will become an powerful device for the usage of the innovative capability of the mind and understanding our desires even as paired with visualization.

The exercise of meditation consists of clearing the thoughts and developing a profoundly attentive and comfortable state. On the alternative hand, visualization is the approach of conjuring up clean, shiny photos within the mind of the supposed results. Meditating and visualizing together produce a effective synergy that synchronizes our thoughts, emotions, and behaviors with our desires.

Make a list of the belongings you want to appear in advance than you begin your meditation and visualization exercising. Give your desires a clean, specific definition. Put them in writing, giving them a real, unyielding perception. When you speak your intentions truly, your subconscious mind turns into extra supportive of the manifestation technique.

a. Locate a Calm and Comfortable Place: Pick a relaxed placing free from interruptions so you can meditate and envision. Whether it is a room set aside for the motive, a serene garden, or a snug corner in your own home, create a sacred location that facilitates your practice. B. Centering and Relaxation: Take some deep breaths and settle into a snug chair to begin your exercise. Let skip of any anxiety or pressure in your body thru way of permitting it to loosen up. Using your breath as an anchor to go again your awareness to the right proper here and now, supply interest to the texture of your breathing.

c. Develop Mindfulness: Bring your interest to the winning 2nd to enter a meditative country. Without passing judgment, sincerely be conscious your thoughts and permit them to bypass thru using like fleeting clouds.

Whenever your mind stray, gently deliver them decrease again on your respiration.

d. Incorporate Visualization: Start the usage of visualization as short as you've got emerge as cushty for your meditative u . S .. Using your creativeness, visualize your intended results definitely to your thoughts. Take have a look at of the colors, paperwork, and records. Enjoy the feelings and proper vibes that include knowing your dreams.

e. Adopt Positive Thoughts: Keep an awesome outlook and repeat affirmations to yourself even as you visualize. Say something empowering to dispel any doubts or constricting thoughts. In different phrases, "I am nicely really worth of my dreams," "I appeal to abundance into my lifestyles," as well as "I am capable of manifesting my private desires."

f. Enhance the Experience: Make your visualization and meditation exercising greater profound with the resource of together with audiovisual aids or guided meditations. You can reputation better and gain your dreams with the aid of the use of these resources, which also can help you loosen up and locate inspiration.

Establish ordinary meditation and visualization wearing events. Allocate a selected length each day to participate on this existence-converting exercise. Maintaining consistency will let you expect surely and assemble a more potent bond along with your desires. You develop extra in music with the manifestation machine the extra often you workout this.

Using meditation to improve visualization is a non violent technique that offers you the capability to consciously and purposefully deliver your wants to life. You may also join your thoughts, emotions, and behaviors with the outcomes you want with the beneficial resource of fusing the profound rest and mindfulness of meditation with vibrant mental photos.

Chapter 13: Aligning Thoughts And Behavior

The Role of Action in Manifestation:

Using the electricity of exceptional thinking, imagery, and movement, manifestation is a dynamic method. Your desires can come actual through inspired motion, however the basis for their manifestation is laid thru incredible perception and visualization. Here are a few useful pointers for using it to help your constructive thinking and firmly and purposefully materialize your dreams.

The spark that turns desires into truth is motion. It serves as a link the various location of intentions and the actualization of your dreams. You can create a robust strain of appeal with the aid of manner of consciously moving within the direction of your goals and bringing your mind, feelings, and ideals into alignment with the outdoor surroundings.

Your movements are propelled through the use of your powerful mind. An remarkable outlook fosters self guarantee on your functionality to hold your desires to life. Having high quality thinking gives upward push to energy, fortitude, and a feel of opportunity—all vital for constantly and creatively acting.

Establish unique, measurable dreams simply so your conduct will reflect your goals. Identify the goals you want to perform. Divide your aspirations into capacity desires and segments. You can live responsible, centered, and inspired with the useful useful resource of putting your dreams in writing and checking them frequently.

Taking Inspired Action: a. Determine Doable Steps: Divide your goals into greater achievable, smaller sports activities. Determine the perfect steps you have to take to get in the direction of your goals. Every movement object need to be precise, quantifiable, and down to earth in fact. You can do sluggish, ordinary sports with this method to benefit momentum.

b. Adopt a Growth Mindset: Use a boom thoughts-set to technique every project. Accept limitations as possibilities for development and education. Consider setbacks as temporary roadblocks as opposed to irreversible disasters. Throughout your manifestation technique, keeping your resilience and motivation is facilitated through adopting a development thoughts-set.

c. Overcoming Resistance: When venturing past your consolation quarter, resistance and fear regularly floor. Understand that those feelings are normal reactions to improvement and trade. Move ahead with bravery, taking tiny steps at a time, understanding that every step receives you inside the route of your desires.

d. Visualize Your Actions: Make positive your movement steps are visually represented. Imagine your self completing the project efficiently and with self warranty in advance than you begin. Envision your self achieving each aim and reaping the blessings. Your conviction that your movements are powerful is bolstered with the resource of manner of this visualization.

e. Celebrate Progress: Take time to apprehend and commemorate every small victory and milestone that you have reached. Realize that your accomplishments are evidence of your willpower and difficult paintings. Celebrating your successes lets in you stay stimulated to maintain shifting in advance with the aid of manner of reinforcing your exceptional attitude.

Be willing to adjust your techniques and actions as you skip along on your manifestation course. Evaluate the effects of your efforts and recall what's powerful and what calls for improvement. To maximize your development within the course of your dreams, be adaptable and prepared to make path corrections.

Perseverance and staying power are essential for manifestation. Remain committed in your goals regardless of issues or disappointments. Remain positive, act normally from idea, and believe inside the technique. Keep in mind that every circulate you are making brings you one step within the course of understanding your dreams.

Chapter 14: Understanding The Science Of Positivity

Discover the mysteries of positivity with the resource of way of delving into the charming fields of neurobiology and psychology. Discover how thinking surely influences the way your mind works, building resilience and changing the chemistry of your mind. Learn the generation underlying the exercise of excellent questioning on this financial disaster, and set up the inspiration for a lifestyles-converting shift within the path of a greater fine outlook.

The Psychology of Positive Thinking

Positive wondering is greater effective than optimism on my own because it explores complicated intellectual areas and influences no longer truly how we recognize matters but additionally the form of our mental health. Imagine the mind as a canvas as we begin this exploration, and high excellent wondering as the incredible paintbrush that creates the masterpiece that is our emotional landscape.

1. Perception's Power to Shape Reality

Thinking certainly impacts our perceptions, affecting how we recognize and react to the surroundings. It's a intellectual phenomenon wherein the mind sees topics greater definitely at the same time as it's far inclined to be extraordinary. Adversity will become a boom catalyst, opportunities upward thrust up from annoying conditions, and setbacks become instructions.

2. Cognitive Restructuring: Reorganizing Mental Processes

Cognitive restructuring, a intellectual technique wherein we deliberately contest and reframe terrible mind, is the muse of fantastic wondering. People can trade the manner they suppose thru recognizing lousy patterns and swapping them out for exceptional ones. This life-converting approach no longer most effective modifies our mentality but additionally the emotional and physical reactions related to various ideas.

3. Neurotransmitters' Function: Positive Chemicals

Positive wondering is a physiological phenomenon in location of just a intellectual thoughts-set. Positive thoughts cause neurotransmitters, commonly known as "sense-authentic" chemical materials like serotonin and dopamine, to spike. These neurochemicals manual a extraordinary feedback loop that will increase intellectual fitness via way of improving mood further to improving cognitive characteristic.

4. Emotional Hardiness: Handling Life's Difficulties

By fostering emotional resilience, positivity serves as a seawall in competition to lifestyles's turbulence. Positive thinkers are psychologically more capable of dealing with strain, getting higher from setbacks, and keeping highbrow stability in attempting occasions. Resilience isn't always a passive excellent; alternatively, it's far a dynamic mental response this is fostered through manner of continuously wondering definitely.

5. Confidence and Self-Efficacy: Developing the Mind

Positive questioning will boom self-efficacy, or the conviction that you could conquer barriers and understand their dreams. This mental empowerment is more than virtually self-assure; it will become the impetus for initiative, tenacity, and openness to opportunities. The highbrow interaction among self-efficacy and exquisite thinking establishes the muse for each career and private achievement.

6. Social and Interpersonal Advantages: Establishing Relationships

Contagious positivity affects our social interactions in a cascading way. Psychologically, first-rate people generally have a tendency to attract special extremely good people to them, which creates more potent bonds and extra alluring relationships.

Positive wondering psychology affects no longer just the psychology of the character but moreover the dynamics of communities and social networks.

7. Holistic Well-Being: The Mind-Body Connection

Positive questioning has highbrow benefits which might be contemplated inside the complicated dance some of the thoughts and body. Numerous medical studies exhibit the beneficial consequences of excessive first-rate questioning on bodily fitness, which include durability, cardiovascular health, and immune system usual ordinary overall performance. Understanding that developing a first rate outlook is a holistic approach to trendy nicely-being is bolstered through the thoughts-frame connection.

Deciphering the psychology of great wondering famous a profound truth: the mind has a splendid capability to influence our reality. Let the knowledge we find out as we find out the depths of this mental phenomenon feature a catalyst for profound transformation, permitting a certainly charged thoughts to attain its complete functionality.

The Effects of Positive Thinking on Mental Health

The advantages of excessive pleasant wondering on intellectual fitness are profound and a long way-achieving, similar to a mild breeze via the lawn of the thoughts. We find out how the intentional sowing of fine seeds can extend right right into a resilient and emotionally strong tapestry as we wind thru this lush landscape.

1. Reducing Stress: Quieting the Inner Storm

Thinking sincerely calms the mind and calms the storms of pressure. Positive attitudes and mind have a robust psychological effect due to the fact they oppose the body's herbal stress response. People can decorate their intellectual fitness with the resource of reducing the bad effects of prolonged-term pressure and developing a first rate thoughts-set.

2. Relieving Anxiety: Calming the Worried Mind

Positive questioning is a powerful weapon in the direction of tension, a commonplace highbrow health trouble. When human beings undertake an tremendous outlook, they face and question their terrible mind and shift their hobby to effective possibilities. Anxiety is weakened psychologically while anticipated threats are modified with effective opportunities, which promotes serenity and mastery.

3. Depression Resilience: Casting Light on the Shadows

Thinking surely serves as a ray of desire while handling melancholy. Cultivating optimism has been verified to enhance resilience in opposition to depressive episodes, despite the fact that it may no longer offer a treatment. Positive questioning creates a intellectual buoyancy that acts as a lifeline, permitting people to extra resiliently experience out the americaand downs of depressive cycles.

4. Bright Hue Painting for Improved Emotional Well-Being

Emotional properly-being is the colorful canvas that is painted with a pleasant thoughts-set. Positive questioning has been associated in research to superior mood, better levels of happiness, and more lifestyles pride. The intellectual uplift delivered approximately via effective thinking contributes to an emotional surroundings that is defined through happiness and fulfillment.

Chapter 15: Overcoming Negative Thought Patterns

Negative concept patterns can weave a spellbinding pattern within the complicated mental fabric. We set out on a transformative adventure in this bankruptcy, exploring numerous techniques to understand, question, and reinterpret those styles.

Understanding the complex intellectual dynamics at art work paves the manner for a extra superb outlook and a more potent intellectual panorama. Let the positivity shine at the manner to powerful transformation as we find out the paintings of conquering terrible concept styles.

Identifying Negative Thought Patterns

Often, negativity can entwine itself inside the course of our minds, impacting our emotions and behaviors. This bankruptcy sets off on a deep journey of self-discovery—a project to reveal the hidden sorts of horrible thinking that may be subconsciously strolling our minds and to discover the shadows.

1. The Structure of Adverse Thought Patterns

Analyzing negativity's anatomy is the first step in the direction of information it. Cognitive distortions, or biased and unreasonable strategies of processing statistics, are common manifestations of awful belief styles. We can studies extra about the underlying reasons of pessimistic questioning, which includes catastrophizing and black-and-white wondering, through dissecting the ones misconceptions.

Uncovering Autonomous Negative Thoughts (ANTs)

Automatic Negative Thoughts (ANTs) are the quick-witted messengers of negativity that can rapid trade our perception. Recognizing the ones reflexive reactions is critical to breaking the terrible comments loop. We discover the arena of ANTs and study their subtle impact on our feelings and actions.

three. Returning to Fundamental Ideas

Negative concept styles often stem from deeply held fundamental beliefs. Our worldview is lengthy-established by way of approach of these mind, that are regularly superior finally of childhood or thru crucial existence tales. A essential first step in converting destructive idea patterns and promoting an optimistic mind-set is spotting and disputing the ones essential assumptions.

4. Identifying Adverse Self-Talk

We have fantastic energy over our inner speak, or the quiet talks we have were given with ourselves. When unchecked, terrible self-communicate can beef up dangerous cognitive conduct. Through introspection and self-interest, we can discover ways to choose out negative self-talk and update it with a type and useful internal conversation.

five. Emotional Response Patterns

Our feelings are like mirrors that mirror the power of our thoughts. Examining the emotional reactions elicited thru particular mind is crucial to discover hard idea patterns. Finding styles in our emotional responses helps us to perceive the subtle symptoms that cause self-recognition and comprehension of our intellectual strategies.

6. Identifying Patterns in Behavior

Beyond the mind, terrible idea patterns show up in our movements. Avoidance, self-sabotage, and procrastination can all be symptoms and symptoms of underlying lousy questioning. Through near assertion of behavioral patterns, we are able to find out how negativity affects our moves and triumph over self-imposed constraints.

7. Using Journals as a Reflective Instrument

Writing in a magazine will become our considerate satisfactory pal in recognizing bad belief patterns. We provide a consistent surroundings for introspection and self-expression even as we mag. Writing down our feelings, mind, and moves famous styles that we won't have determined in any other case, giving us a concrete documentation of our development closer to self-attention.

Let this research feature a lighthouse for self-discovery as we got all the way down to picks out out detrimental idea styles. By developing our self-cognizance, we open the door to confronting and reforming those styles, it's far a important first step in embracing positivity's shiny slight.

Click the hyperlink underneath to buy the paperback model of this e-book at a reduced fee as it carries greater notes to Jot down your Observation and experience.

Chapter 16: Cultivating A Positive Mindset

Maintaining a glad outlook is like taking care of a blossoming lawn inside the extensive landscape that is the mind. It desires cautious interest, beneficial art work, and a deep comprehension of the highbrow concepts that aid optimism. This financial catastrophe reads like a roadmap, taking the reader on a ride through the wealthy soil of optimism, in which hopeful seeds are planted and become colourful blooms.

1. Expressing Gratitude: The Foundation for Happiness

Gratitude is the rich soil that is at the center of developing an extraordinary outlook. We explore the remodeling functionality of thankfulness practices, inspecting how recognising and valuing existence's excellent matters can function catalysts for a exchange in point of view. As the muse, gratitude creates the surroundings for developing an sufficient and appreciative mind-set.

2. Awareness of the Present Moment and Mindfulness

The canvas on which the fabric of our lifestyles is sewn is the winning immediately. Being conscious turns into the paintbrush with which every moment is deliberately and mindfully painted. We dissect the intellectual nuances of mindfulness, investigating how being surely gift grounds us in the richness of each revel in, which promotes an high-quality outlook.

three. Positive Self-Talk and Affirmations

The narrative of our intellectual fact is customary with the resource of the terms we are pronouncing to ourselves, every spoken and unsaid. Affirmations and amazing self-communicate show up as powerful techniques for growing an fantastic outlook. We observe the psychology of affirmations, identifying that planned language has the power to transform our attitudes, ideals, and ultimately our fact.

4. Adopting Positive Thought Patterns

Thinking in an best manner is like planting seeds for a powerful mindset. We check the subtleties of pleasant wondering, together with cultivating a perception in oneself to triumph over problems and viewing boundaries as possibilities. To cultivate the ones styles, one should confront negativity, reframe viewpoints, and undertake an answer-focused mind-set.

five. Positive Visualization's Effect

Positive visualization is the abilities of portray a shiny future on the canvas this is the creativeness. We explore how vividly visualizing glad consequences improves motivation, self warranty, and the general trajectory of our endeavors as we delve into the mental advantages of powerful visualization. With the strength of aim, visualization will become a device for developing a first-rate outlook.

6. Generosity and Benevolence

Being type is like having a vivid moderate shining right down to your inner seeds of optimism. We observe the intellectual underpinnings of compassion and generosity, comprehending the techniques wherein these deeds useful resource an splendid outlook. Fostering optimism thru charitable deeds no longer satisfactory makes others happier however moreover affords happiness and satisfaction for the most effective doing the giving.

7. Establishing a Conducive Setting

The putting wherein our mind first emerge may be very essential for developing a outstanding outlook. We dissect the psychological consequences of surrounding oneself with notable matters, whether or not or not in interpersonal interactions, interior design, or media utilization. Fostering a useful surroundings will become vital to retaining an constructive outlook.

Chapter 17: Nurturing Positive Relationships

Relationships provide the history in competition to which our memories play out within the complex dance of lifestyles. Building healthy relationships calls for a cautious stability of shared recollections, verbal exchange, and feelings. It is each an art work and a technological knowledge. This financial ruin takes you on a adventure into the middle of connection, in which enduring ties, achievement, and know-how are woven together through wonderful threads.

1. Positive Communication's Fundamentals

Relationships rely on communication, and positive communique builds emotional bridges throughout divides in opinion. We find out the subtleties of encouraging amazing conversation, paying interest, and expressing gratitude. Good relationships are constructed on a foundation of positive verbal exchange, which serves as its cornerstone.

2. Thanking and displaying appreciation

Gratitude is the unsaid language of the coronary heart, and showing it to others may also have a profoundly tremendous impact on relationships. We check how appreciation and thankfulness feature keeping fluids, developing a area in which humans sense seen, liked, and recounted. Intentional acts of gratitude foster the increase and improvement of useful connections.

three. Establishing Empathy: The Vital Sign of Bonding

Understanding and connection are based mostly on empathy. We dissect the highbrow factors of empathy, analyzing how the functionality to location oneself in every other person's shoes cultivates robust emotional ties. Fostering empathy turns will become a guiding precept for constructing wholesome bonds with others, fostering an environment this is conducive to compassion and knowledge.

four. Modifiable Conflict Settlement

Any dating will continually have conflict, however how we control it determines how our dating develops. We discover the functionality of high-quality warfare selection, comprehending the highbrow strategies that turn arguments into studying stories. Good partnerships construct know-how and resilience with the resource of gracefully navigating boundaries.

five. Generosity and Consideration

Tiny acts of kindness have the electricity to unfold optimism sooner or later of relationships. We check out the highbrow effects of thoughtfulness and compassion, realising how these deeds help a loving and appreciative society. A regular act of kindness goes an prolonged manner inside the route of fostering strong relationships with the useful resource of fostering a happy and supportive surroundings.

6. Spending Time Together and Exchanging Stories

Positive relationships are built on the foundation of extremely good time spent collectively. We dissect the intellectual charge of shared testimonies and test out how deep connections produce enduring recollections. Building a reservoir of shared happiness and data through planned moments of connection is vital to nurturing first-rate relationships.

7. Fostering Personal Development in Relationships

Good connections offer a wealthy surroundings for non-public development. We communicate how uplifting every different's dreams, promoting self-improvement, and cultivating a feel of independence all result in the boom of healthful relationships. Maintaining healthful partnerships requires hanging a careful stability among mutual dreams and private improvement.

EMBRACING RESILIENCE AND GROWTH

Growth is the sluggish unfolding of our capability within the face of hardship, and resilience is the silent strength that lets in us to climate life's storms. We skip on a deep studies in this financial catastrophe—a adventure into the furnace of wonderful trade. It's a path of accepting issues, building resilience, and tending to the rich soil that produces growth in every relationships and oneself.

1. Resilience's Nature: Dancing with Adversity

The functionality to conquer obstacles gracefully is what defines resilience, now not the dearth of problems. We explore the mental additives of resilience, reading how the human mind handles trouble. Developing an thoughts-set that sees failures as opportunities for improvement and reinterprets barriers as stepping stones closer to one's very personal development is critical to embracing resilience.

2. Recovering from Failures: The Alchemical Process of Adversity

Failures are possibilities to expand and trade, no longer barriers to be triumph over. We study the intellectual alchemy that happens at the same time as we method adversities with a increase-orientated angle and an open heart. Accepting defeats turns them right right into a reading enjoy in which limitations characteristic teachers of self-cognizance, resiliency, and redoubled treatment.

three. How Self-Reflection Aids in Personal Development

The mirror of self-mirrored picture permits us to look ourselves and our thoughts, actions, and desires. We explore the mental benefits of self-mirrored image in selling improvement. Accepting self-reflected image makes it a planned exercise that facilitates us higher apprehend who we're, pinpoint areas in which we may moreover broaden, and boom an ongoing device of self-discovery.

4. Cultivating a Growth Attitude

The wealthy soil from which non-public and interpersonal growth emerges is a boom mentality. We have a take a look at the mental components of growing a increase attitude, that's an outlook that views limitations as chances to develop and have a study. Reframing limiting beliefs, growing interest, and fostering the thoughts-set that there is commonly room for development are all a part of adopting a increase thoughts-set.

five. Fostering Relationship Resilience

Resilience and high-quality courting transformation are carefully associated. We discover the intellectual dynamics that have an effect on every relational and individual resilience, identifying that overcoming boundaries together strengthens bonds. Embracing resilience in partnerships entails a shared dedication to progress, real communique in the route of hard times, and mutual help.

6. Adapting and Growing inside the Face of Uncertainty

Uncertainty coexists with change as a consistent. We have a look at the highbrow components of thriving within the face of uncertainty and change, identifying the jobs that resilience and flexibility play in fostering constructive development. Accepting trade creates a mindset that perspectives shifts as possibilities for rejuvenation, flexibility as a strength, and ambiguity as a blank canvas for easy mind.

7. Promoting an Environment of Constant Enhancement

Progress is a manner in preference to an end motive. We dissect the mental underpinnings of creating a life-style of ongoing development on an person and interpersonal degree. Setting goals, acknowledging accomplishments, and preserving an optimistic outlook that values the unceasing adventure of turning into the top notch versions of us are all a part of embracing continual increase.

May this bankruptcy feature a beacon of choice and guidance for us as we traverse the panorama of accepting development and resilience? It gives belief, useful advice, and a deep comprehension of the highbrow nuances that underlie right transformation. I desire your course is one in every of resiliency, improvement, and the persevering with popularity of your boundless ability.

Chapter 18: Creating A Positive Environment

Environments are more than in reality bodily locations; they represent the complex net of emotions, thoughts, and forces that have an effect on how we stay our lives. This chapter takes us on an intentional revolutionary adventure, delving into the art work and technological know-how of making satisfied surroundings. It's a portray in which optimism serves because the ancient beyond painter for lives which can be thriving.

1. Physical Spaces' Power to Shape Atmosphere and Mood

Our environment has a massive effect on how we experience. We examine the psychology of physical environments, gaining knowledge of how layout abilties like shade, lighting, and layout have an effect on our emotions. A fantastic surroundings is the stop result of planned layout choices that foster perception, peace of thoughts, and stylish health.

2. Cultivating Positivity in Relationships

Relationships are important components of our environmental international. We delve into the mental elements of constructing super connections, spotting how the quality of interactions notably determines our emotional climate. Creating a pleasant surroundings in partnerships consists of open verbal exchange, mutual guide, and the intentional cultivation of joy and facts.

three. Media Consumption and Positivity

The media we consume becomes the story that defines our attitude. We take a look at the mental effect of media intake on our intellectual environment, recognizing the have an effect on it bears on our attitudes and feelings. Creating a first-rate media environment includes intentional picks, discernment, and a beneficial try and interact with facts that uplifts and conjures up.

four. The Role of Daily Habits and Routines

Habits and workout routines are the everyday heartbeat of our every day life. We solve the mental implications of constructing exceptional conduct and workout routines, explaining how they make contributions to a sense of shape, purpose, and preferred optimism. Creating a wholesome environment through regular practices includes conscious alternatives that healthy with our ideals and well-being.

five. Bringing Nature into Your Space

Nature, with its intrinsic beauty and peace, has a great effect on our mental situation. We take a look at out the psychology of infusing nature into our environment, gaining knowledge of how green areas, natural elements, and outdoor reviews make a contribution to a healthful thoughts-set. Creating a nice surroundings with nature approach bringing factors of the outside internal and consciously spending time in herbal settings.

6. Decluttering the Mind and Physical Space

Clutter, whether or not or now not highbrow or bodily, can generate a revel in of false impression. We dig into the highbrow blessings of decluttering—each our minds and physical areas. Creating a satisfied surroundings via decluttering technique letting circulate of useless luggage, arranging our surrounds, and promoting a revel in of simplicity and readability.

7. Infusing Positivity into Daily Interactions

Every interaction is an possibility to contribute to the emotional climate of our environment. We have a look at the psychology of useful encounters, know-how how gestures, words, and attitudes have an effect at the entire environment. Creating a immoderate awesome environment through every day encounters consists of exercising compassion, empathy, and aware efforts to uplift people spherical us.

As we find out the panorama of building a exquisite environment, can also moreover this financial smash be a manual—a deliver of concept, realistic insights, and a profound draw close of the mental standards that assist the realistic development of positivity. May your environment end up a masterpiece, reflecting the splendor, peace, and flourishing lifestyles that unfold interior its consist of.

SUSTAINING POSITIVITY IN THE LONG TERM

Being immoderate high-quality is a rustic of being that can be advanced and maintained over time, rather than a brief emotion. This monetary smash takes us on a adventure through the behaviors, attitudes, and intellectual ideas that contribute to the iconic brightness of a extremely good existence—an exam of the art work and technology of prolonged-term positivity.

1. Long-Term Positive Psychology

It is essential to recognize the psychological foundations of prolonged-term positivity. We test the foundational thoughts of effective psychology and the way useful practices, conduct, and thoughts-set affect prolonged-term properly-being. The mystery to lengthy-term positivism is to create a intellectual environment wherein feeling applicable is everyday and a part of each day life.

2. Daily Positive Rituals

Our lives are rhythmic dances that we name rituals. We check out the psychology of imposing exceptional workout routines into our day by day lives, seeing how the ones planned actions grow to be moorings inside the americaand downs of our days. Making rituals that assist a experience of cause and pleasure and are ordinary with personal values is critical to prolonged-term positivity sustainability.

3. The Foundation of Long-Term Positive Thinking: Resilience

The basis of resilience is what makes prolonged-lasting positivity possible. We discover the mental underpinnings of resilience and the way overcoming obstacles promotes prolonged-term properly being.

Maintaining optimism includes constructing a resilient mind-set that sees failures as probabilities for improvement, strengthening the emotional basis for lengthy-term achievement.

4. Mindful Living: The Remedy for Superfluous Stress

Being actually found in each moment is the capability of mindfulness. We have a look at the mental benefits of conscious residing, comprehending the way it fosters inner calm and acts as a counterbalance to useless tension. Long-time period amazing renovation requires incorporating mindfulness into every day residing and cultivating a peaceful, alert highbrow environment.

5. Ongoing Education and Development

The quest for information and self-improvement is an limitless deliver of idea. We discover the psychology of lifelong mastering, knowledge how progress and interest result in a happy and fulfilled existence. Maintaining optimism entails adopting a lifelong gaining knowledge of thoughts-set in which every occasion is regarded as a risk for intellectual and personal boom.

6. Juggling Contribution and Self-Care

A continual incredible outlook is genuinely approximately putting a careful balance amongst self-care and giving once more. We have a look at the psychology of attaining stability and the manner looking after oneself and supporting others can also cause a happy life. Maintaining positivity involves making conscious efforts to appearance after one's health and actively taking element in deeds of compassion and provider.

7. Fostering Good Relationships and Support Systems

In the ocean of life, healthful connections feature anchors. We dissect the mental significance of constructing healthy relationships and help systems and recognise how they beautify prolonged-term fitness. Maintaining optimism consists of cultivating deep connections wherein knowledge, pleasure, and resource for each one-of-a-kind become vital components of the direction.

May this financial destroy function a compass for us as we traverse the terrain of extended-time period splendid protection—a roadmap supplying know-how, possible strategies, and an in-intensity comprehension of the mental thoughts that form the inspiration of the art work of tolerating brightness.

I preference your course is one in every of unwavering optimism, in which each day serves as a easy canvas on which to coloration a colorful and pleasing existence.

Chapter 19: Understanding Success

Success is a time period that holds distinct meanings for excellent human beings. Some may additionally furthermore see success as accomplishing their desires and achieving the pinnacle of their profession, at the same time as others can also view success as living a satisfied and fulfilled life. Regardless of approaches one defines fulfillment, it's far a full-size desire for everybody to obtain it. However, the journey to fulfillment isn't always normally easy and easy. It requires information, strength of mind, and the right attitude to end up your exceptional self and acquire what you prefer.

What is Success?

As mentioned earlier, the definition of success varies from person to character. However, a commonplace information of success is the accomplishment of dreams that bring a enjoy of satisfaction, contentment, and fulfillment. These desires may be in any hassle of existence, consisting of career, relationships, personal development, fitness, or spirituality. It is important to phrase that success is a subjective idea, and what may be considered a fulfillment for one person might not be the same for some other.

Factors Affecting Success

Various factors can also have an impact on an character's adventure within the path of success. These can encompass their upbringing, training, belongings, surroundings, and possibilities. While some can also have access to all of the vital belongings and possibilities, others may additionally moreover have to paintings more difficult and triumph over extra significant demanding situations to obtain success. However, one key element that plays a essential function in identifying success is an character's thoughts-set. The Role of Mindset in Success

The thoughts-set, or one's mind-set and ideals in the course of oneself and the world, has a sizable effect on success. People with a growth thoughts-set receive as real with that they're capable of increase their competencies and intelligence via strength of will and tough work, therefore giving them the motivation to pursue their desires however limitations. On the opportunity hand, humans with a hard and fast attitude remember that their competencies and intelligence are steady and can't be changed or progressed upon, foremost to a loss of motivation and a fear of failure.

A increase mindset is vital for undertaking fulfillment as it permits people to look traumatic conditions and setbacks as opportunities to look at and grow, whilst a difficult and rapid mind-set can inhibit private growth and development. Therefore, it's far critical to cultivate a boom thoughts-set and exercise self-cognizance to end up aware about and triumph over limiting ideals that would hinder achievement.

Defining Your Own Version of Success

With societal strain and expectancies, it is simple to fall into the trap of pursuing a person else's idea of achievement. However, fulfillment is private and subjective, and it's miles important to outline what it way to you. It is vital to take some time to reflect to your values, passions, and dreams in life and outline achievement in step with them. This will let you have a clean information of what you want to benefit and why it is vital to you.

The Journey to Success

Success isn't a vacation spot however a journey. It is a non-prevent machine of increase, studying, and variation. It calls for willpower, tough paintings, and resilience. Often, human beings can also face failures, setbacks, and challenges on their route to fulfillment, but it's far how they cope with those boundaries that decide their achievement. Perseverance, grit, and resilience are essential developments to have on the adventure to fulfillment. It is crucial to undergo in mind that failure is a natural part of the adventure, and it want to no longer discourage one from pursuing their dreams. Instead, failure want to be visible as a reading enjoy and an possibility to reconsider and beautify. Successful human beings regularly have a boom mind-set and be aware disasters as stepping stones toward fulfillment.

Defining and Celebrating Milestones

On the journey to success, it's far critical to have amusing small victories and milestones. Setting and reaching smaller desires along the manner can decorate motivation and offer a revel in of fulfillment and improvement. It is crucial to well known and have a laugh those milestones, no matter how small, to live inspired and maintain going inside the path of the last motive.

Definition of fulfillment to My angle

Like I said earlier than, achievement may be defined in lots of strategies, but to my mind-set, it's far the technique of becoming your outstanding self, each in mindset and motivation. It isn't pretty much achieving desires or acquiring cloth possessions, however as an alternative, a non-stop adventure of personal increase and self-improvement.

To start with, achievement begins with having the right mind-set. This way having a high-quality and high quality outlook on life, and believing to your very very personal competencies and ability. It moreover includes being self-conscious, know-how your strengths and weaknesses, and constantly searching out techniques to decorate and examine from disasters. A a success person is constantly open to new mind, willing to take dangers and step out of their consolation sector, and has a boom thoughts-set that sees demanding situations as possibilities for boom.

In addition, motivation is important for success. It is the using strain that keeps us going in the direction of our desires and desires. A prompted man or woman is passionate and decided, and has a easy vision of what they want to benefit. They are not with out trouble discouraged via manner of setbacks or obstacles, however instead, use them as fuel to maintain jogging in the direction of their desires.

Becoming your exquisite self also method having a strong enjoy of cause. This includes expertise your values, passions, and what without a doubt makes you satisfied, and aligning them together along side your desires. When your movements are consistent together together with your cause, success becomes extra enormous and proper.

Furthermore, achievement isn't a one-time achievement, but a non-forestall adventure. It isn't always enough to gain a high best stage of fulfillment after which save you striving for introduced. A in fact a achievement character is typically searching out development and boom, constantly setting new desires and disturbing situations for themselves. They apprehend that fulfillment isn't always a destination but a in no way-ending system.

However, it's also important to bear in mind that achievement isn't quite a whole lot the character however additionally about creating a super effect on others and the area. A a achievement character makes use of their abilities and assets to uplift and inspire others, developing a ripple impact of positivity and achievement

Explore the specific definitions and interpretations of fulfillment

Success. A phrase that incorporates with it a myriad of meanings and interpretations. Some can also companion it with wealth and cloth possessions, on the identical time as others might also moreover additionally view it as undertaking private dreams and achievement. But what does achievement in reality mean? Is there best one definition or can or not it is interpreted in numerous strategies? Let's delve deeper into this complex but thrilling concept via one among a kind lenses.

For a few, fulfillment is synonymous with attaining the top of the organisation ladder. Climbing the rungs of success, accumulating wealth and attaining a immoderate recognition in society. This mind-set is often bolstered thru societal pressures and media portrayals of success. A story that exemplifies this interpretation of achievement is that of John.

John had normally been bold, driven with the resource of a desire to climb the company ladder and advantage financial fulfillment. He worked tirelessly, installing lengthy hours and sacrificing personal relationships for his interest. Slowly but simply, he rose thru the ranks and have grow to be a pinnacle government in his corporation. He lived in a high priced penthouse, drove a fancy vehicle and changed into surrounded with the aid of way of fabric wealth. On the floor, John may also have regarded to be a successful guy, however as time went on, he found out that some issue emerge as lacking. Despite his wealth, he felt unfulfilled and yearned for a deeper feel of purpose and that means in his existence.

On the other hand, a few human beings define success as attaining personal goals and locating happiness and fulfillment of their every day lives. This interpretation of fulfillment isn't tied to fabric possessions or societal expectancies, but instead to one's very very own aspirations and enjoy of cause.

A story that embodies this attitude is that of Maria. Maria modified right into a simple girl, content material cloth along facet her modest assignment and clean manner of lifestyles.

www.ingramcontent.com/pod-product-compliance
Lightning Source LLC
Chambersburg PA
CBHW072157070526
44585CB00015B/1185